Guided Enactments in Psychoanalytic Psychotherapy

Psychodynamic Psychotherapy and Assessment in the Twenty-First Century

Series Editor

Steven Tuber, City University of New York at City College

Psychodynamic Psychotherapy and Assessment in the Twenty-First Century establishes a milieu for the presentation of scholarly clinical work through a developmental lens. The emphasis throughout the series is on the integration of scholarship and practice through writings that are informed by both sources of learning. This domain includes works that document both evidence-based and traditional approaches within the field and applies these approaches to work with infants, children, adolescents, and adults. Efforts that link assessment to treatment are especially welcome, as are integrations between neuropsychological (brain-based) and psychological (mind- or self-based) formulations about personality development and its aberrations. The impact of trauma, both chronic and acute, on the psychological lives of its victims is also an important area of study within this domain. New voices within the field are encouraged to write about the interface between the content and process of their emergent thinking and practice. In addition to the areas mentioned above, more experienced clinical scholars are encouraged to write about the supervisory process and its impact on both theory and practice. Works that focus on specific developmental processes and paradigms at points throughout the lifespan are another welcome area for contributions.

Titles in the Series

Guided Enactments in Psychoanalytic Psychotherapy: A New Look at Therapy with Adults and Children, by Sebastiano Santostefano

Guided Enactments in Psychoanalytic Psychotherapy

A New Look at Therapy with Adults and Children

Sebastiano Santostefano

LEXINGTON BOOKS
Lanham • Boulder • New York • London

Published by Lexington Books
An imprint of The Rowman & Littlefield Publishing Group, Inc.
4501 Forbes Boulevard, Suite 200, Lanham, Maryland 20706
www.rowman.com

Unit A, Whitacre Mews, 26-34 Stannary Street, London SE11 4AB

British Library Cataloguing in Publication Information Available

Library of Congress Cataloging-in-Publication Data

Library of Congress Control Number: 2017945466

ISBN 978-1-4985-6100-6 (cloth : alk. paper)
ISBN 978-1-4985-6101-3 (electronic)

Printed in the United States of America

Contents

Preface

In the opinion of several authors noted in chapter 1, interest in psychoanalytic psychotherapy is declining because techniques dominate, such as free associating, discussing feelings, and analyzing dreams. Other authors have reported that about thirty percent of persons do not benefit from psychoanalytic psychotherapy or drop out of therapy prematurely. To address these issues, I propose that concepts from other fields of psychology, that define particular processes, should be integrated into relational psychotherapy. These concepts provide a therapist with a model that identifies adults and children who would not benefit from traditional psychoanalytic psychotherapy, and also provide a sequence of therapeutic techniques that promote positive development in these persons. One of the concepts addresses the meanings and emotions produced by body experiences a person has during childhood that form the foundation of a person's self. These early body-based meanings and emotions influence how a person's cognition and behaviors respond to and interact with persons and environments during adolescence and adulthood. In this preface I share embodied meanings I experienced from childhood to the beginning of my professional career that influenced my interest in this concept. These experiences also influenced the research I conducted for several years, and the theoretical model I developed.

I have always been interested in how the body *speaks*, expressing meanings and related emotions. The roots of this interest derive from my experiences throughout childhood and adolescence. I grew up in a community located in central Connecticut that was established by Sicilians who came from the same village in Sicily (Santostefano, 2012). In addition to using words, these immigrants always used body language as a way of "talking" and expressing meanings and emotions; for example, gestures, facial expressions, body postures, and movements (e.g., Munari, 2005). When I entered the doctoral program in clinical psychology at Pennsylvania State University in 1953, these early experiences with body language became the source of my interest in demonstrating how a person's body expresses meanings and related emotions. Because projective tests and questionnaires dominated at the time as methods to assess meanings-emotions, and still do, the research program I proposed for my doctoral dissertation was initially viewed by the faculty as "strange," but eventually approved. I designed "The Miniature Situations Test" to explore assessing meanings-emotions expressed by the body. This procedure consisted of forty one "miniature situations." With each situation material was placed on a tabletop that permitted two enactments, and the participant was invited to perform whichever one he/she wanted to do.

For my doctoral dissertation, I administered the Miniature Situations Test individually to one hundred and fifty male high school students randomly selected from two high schools. Each student was asked to choose and enact one of the two actions each situation presented, and encouraged to make use of the feelings he experienced when presented each item. To control for position preference, the games were placed on the table before one half of the students in specified left-right positions and reversed for the other half. With one set of items, the student was asked to physically engage one of the two objects placed before him (e.g., break a light bulb or water a plant; use a brush to sweep sawdust scattered on a board, or scatter sawdust on another board; place a hand in a box to explore what might be inside or look at a picture concealed in a folder; scribble on a sheet of paper or erase a line drawn on another sheet). With another set of items the student was asked either to engage the examiner's body or have the examiner engage the student's body (e.g., listen to the examiner's heart with a stethoscope or have the examiner listen to the student's heart; read a brief paragraph to the examiner or have the examiner read the paragraph to the student; place handcuffs on the examiner's wrists or have the examiner place the handcuffs on the student's wrists). With a third set of situations the student was asked to enact on the examiner's body in one of two ways (e.g., tie the examiner's wrists with a rope or slip a pair of gloves over the examiner's hands).

When I correlated the enactments the students performed, the results illustrated that the meanings and emotions they expressed with their bodies were consistent. For example, students who broke a small light bulb rather than a large one also watered a plant instead of breaking a light bulb, swept sawdust scattered on a board instead of scattering sawdust on another board, listened to the examiner's heart with a stethoscope instead of having the examiner listen to the student's heart, and slipped gloves on the examiner's hands instead of tying the examiner's wrists with a rope. I also had the opportunity to hold brief, individual meetings with the teachers to learn their opinions about how the students behaved and related in their classroom. What the teachers shared illustrated that the enactments the students performed were consistent with their general style of relating and interacting. For example the students who, instead of breaking a light bulb, watered a plant, also slipped gloves on the examiner's hands, read a paragraph to the examiner, and listened to the examiner's heart with a stethoscope were described by teachers as outgoing, friendly, and helpful to classmates with homework. Sometimes when a teacher was about to distribute paperwork, these students asked if they could help. The students who had enacted the alternative of each of these situations were usually described as not outgoing and friendly.

My dissertation was published three years after I received my Ph.D. (Santostefano, 1960).

After graduating I entered a two year postdoctoral program in clinical child psychology at the University of Colorado Medical Center. As part of the program I was invited to participate in research programs being conducted by several psychoanalysts (e.g., Rene Spitz, John Benjamin) who gave me the opportunity to continue exploring the miniature situation method to assess the expression of embodied meanings. As one example, in a study of monozygotic twin children, I asked each twin (with the other absent) to stand on one of two wooden boxes that were identical except that one box was half the height of the other. The enactments each pair of twins performed expressed embodied meanings predicting which twin was dominant and which deferent in their relationship, an issue determined later in treatment sessions (e.g., the dominant twins stood up on the taller box).

During the following years I continued exploring the Miniature Situation Test method with various populations: (A) the embodied expressions-enactments of public-school, orphaned, and brain-damaged children (Santostefano, 1965a). The following are examples of the results. Public-school children drew a design free hand rather than trace another design, while brain-damaged children elected to trace the design rather than draw the other freehand. Public school children more often took a drink from a cup rather than from a baby bottle, while orphaned children more often drank from the baby bottle. Orphaned children watered a plant rather than break a light bulb, while brain-damaged children broke a light bulb rather than water a plant; (B) the embodied expressions—enactments of two groups of institutionalized delinquents (Santostefano and Wilson, 1968). One group was housed in a maximum-security building, referred to as the "Cell House," because they had demonstrated inadequate ability to manage the rules of the institution. The other group was housed in a unit referred to as the "Honor Dormitory" because they had demonstrated sufficient responsibility and behavioral control. Significant differences in the enactments performed by these groups when responding to the Miniature Situation Test were observed. For example, Cell House delinquents tied the examiner's wrists with a rope, while Honor Dormitory delinquents slipped gloves over his hands; Cell House delinquents broke the large light bulb, while Honor Dormitory delinquents broke the small light bulb; Cell House delinquents scribbled on a sheet of paper, while Honor Dormitory delinquents erased a line drawn on another sheet of paper. (C) The embodied expressions-enactments of a child and mother when interacting (Santostefano, 1968a). With some situations the child decided how to enact on the mother. For example, the child chose to guide the mother's hand through a maze, while mother held a pencil and closed her eyes, or have the mother guide the child's hand while the child held a pencil and closed her eyes; the child placed a necklace around the mother's neck or tied an apron around the mother's waist. With other situations the mother decided how the child should enact on objects. For example, the mother decided to have the child repair a torn sheet of paper, or have the child tear up and discard another sheet of paper. With another set of situations the mother decided whether she would enact on the child or an object, for example place a Band-Aid on the child's hand or arrange flowers in a vase. In this study patients at a child guidance clinic, and their mother and siblings, were administered situations to gather information that would serve treating the referred child. As one example of the results, a mother presented her seven-year-old daughter, Jane, to the clinic because she is doing poorly in school and is immature. In one session the mother and Jane were administered situations. In a separate meeting the mother and Jane's six-year-old sister, Helen, were also administered situations. As one example of the results, each child chose to have mother guide them through a maze. When Jane closed her eyes and held the pencil so mother could guide her through the maze, mother held the top of the pencil, moved it stiffly, made no contact with Jane's hand and expressed no comments when the maze was completed. In contrast when mother guided Helen through the maze, mother held her hand, gently moved it through the maze, and smiled and commented while Helen laughed. Also after Helen completed the maze, mother spontaneously noted that Helen does excellent work in school. These studies and others resulted in my being invited by an international encyclopedia to submit an historical review of the method of situational testing (Santostefano, 1968b).

The roots of another concept I address in this volume derived from other experiences (i.e., the key role a patient's cognitive processes play in a therapist deciding when and why to prescribe and initiate an enactment in psychotherapy). The cognitive concepts and methods I use emerged from what became known as the "New Look" in cognitive science (Blake and Ramsey, 1951). Elaborated in chapter 3, the New Look approach challenged the focus of cognitive research on "information processing" and emphasized the need to assess the interrelation between cognitive and emotional processes. The New Look was launched by three conferences. One took place at the University of Colorado where, as noted earlier, I participated in a postdoctoral clinical psychology program and then served on the staff. George Klein and Herbert Schlesinger, both psychologists-psychoanalysts, played a key role in launching the New Look approach. They presented research to support their cognitive concept of "perceptual attitudes" that coordinated information from environments and from the person's meanings-emotions, a concept Klein later termed *cognitive control*. In one study, for example, they asked participants who were World War II refuges to estimate the size of each of a series of discs by adjusting a variable circle. On each disc was placed a symbol (e.g., a swastika) the subject was asked to ignore but that provoked emotions-meanings. They observed that participants made greater errors in size estimation with discs containing symbols that provoked particular meanings-emotions. Accordingly they inferred that the meanings-emotions of particular symbols were not being adequately regulated by the cognitive process involved (i.e., focusing attention on information defined as relevant and subordinating irrelevant information). I was introduced to George Klein and David Rappaport and had the benefit of participating in several discussions with them. Stimulated by Klein's concept of cognitive controls and related methods, and because he had focused on the cognitive functioning of adults, I constructed several cognitive tests to explore how many different processes account for the ways in which children and adolescents use information, while regulating personal meanings-emotions, as they negotiate the demands of environments. In addition to evaluating age differences (e.g., Santostefano, 1964a), the procedures investigated the cognitive-emotional functioning of various clinical populations, such as boys who been apprehended while intoxicated from sniffing glue (Dodds and Santostefano, 1964); differences among brain damaged, orphaned, and public-school children (Santostefano, 1964b). This research resulted in my constructing a battery of cognitive tests that assessed how cognition regulates information-emotions, and also resulted in my designing treatment programs to rehabilitate the cognitive functioning of children (e.g., Santostefano, 1978, 1988).

Other personal experiences contributed to the roots of another concept I address in this volume, namely how particular aspects of a patient's developmental history contribute to a therapist deciding when and why to initiate an enactment. In 1964 I moved to Boston to begin training in adult and child psychoanalysis at the Boston Psychoanalytic Institute. While serving on the faculty of Clark University, I learned from other faculty (e.g., Heinz Werner and Seymour Wapner) about the organismic-developmental viewpoint that conceptualized developmental levels in terms of the relations between body experiences and cognitive-emotional functioning. Their developmental viewpoint also advocated that earlier embodied meanings are not replaced by later meanings but become integrated within them (e.g., Werner, 1957). In addition, while I served on the faculty of Clark University, Jean Piaget was invited to conduct a colloquium about his research with infants that contributed to my growing interest in psychological development. Then I was asked to serve on the faculty of Boston University School of Medicine where I collaborated with Louis Sander, a psychoanalyst, who focused on developmental issues related to mother-child interactions (e.g., Sander, 1962, 1964) and whose model is detailed in chapter 3.

My experiences with situational testing, the organismic-developmental viewpoint, psychoanalytically oriented infant research, and my training in psychoanalysis converged, resulting in my first conceptualization of the dialectical relations among embodied meanings, cognition, emotions, and environments (e.g., Santostefano, 1977, 1986). In addition, based on these experiences I also proposed that psychotherapists should move beyond nosology and diagnose from the viewpoint of development (Santostefano, 1971), that principles of infant development could be a useful guide in conducting psychotherapy with children (Santostefano and Berkowitz, 1976), and that therapists should address cognitive functioning within personality functioning (Santostefano, 1980).

After I completed training in adult and child psychoanalysis and assumed the position of Director, Department of Child and Adolescent Psychology at McLean Hospital/Harvard Medical School, I continued conducting psychotherapy and psychoanalysis with children and adults and research that explored the relations among enactments-actions, cognition, meanings, and emotions (e.g., Santostefano, 1985; Santostefano and Moncata, 1989; Santostefano and Rieder, 1984). These projects lead to my emphasizing that the relationship established by a child and therapist, and their enactments, are the catalysts for change, rather than interpretation and self-talk (Santostefano and Calicchia, 1992).

My interest in the fourth concept I address in this volume was also launched in childhood experiences (Santostefano, 1998a); i.e., that usual and unusual environments require particular cognitive-emotional processes and behaviors in order for a person to cope successfully, and that environments play a role in making available opportunities to construct, express and revise embodied meanings. For example, while torrential rain pounded outside, my siblings and I were huddled around the radio listening to an episode of "Jack Armstrong," as our mother prepared dinner. Our father was standing at the back door of our apartment, taking a breath of fresh air. Suddenly he called out to us in our native Sicilian dialect to come quickly so we can see an example of how much the environment could help if we use it in a way that fits what we need. As we huddled around the doorway, he pointed to a large cat standing in a patch of tall weeds. From the cat's mouth dangled a very small kitten by the back of its neck. The cat turned from side to side desperately looking for a safe place. Suddenly the cat raced across the patch of ground and jumped into a barrel that had tipped over. The cat stepped out of the barrel without the kitten, ran across the patch of ground, picked up another kitten buried in the patch of tall weeds and raced back to the barrel. She repeated this two more times. As we all exclaimed, my father commented that if you use the outdoors in the right way, there are solutions to the storms of life. Apparently my father was good at helping people deal with the storms of life. Our neighborhood was populated by immigrants from the same village in Sicily. Each Sunday afternoon, sometimes a couple, or a father and his son or daughter, or a mother and her son or daughter, or a family would visit our apartment and sit in our small parlor, engaging in a discussion or intense argument. My father, I learned later, provided a service that his father had provided in the Sicilian village, namely using the environment to negotiate problems. I noticed, for example, that after a discussion with one father and his son, he asked them to go to the nearby river and compete who could throw a rock the farthest into the river. As another example, he recommended to a mother and daughter that they take a walk through the bushes by the river, and while holding hands touch the leaves with the other hand.

These experiences influenced how I served in the army before entering college. After I completed high school, I enlisted in the United States Army because the World War II draft was still active. If you enlisted, you could select to which branch you would be assigned after basic training. I had elected to serve in the medics. After basic training, I was trained to be a medic and assigned to a station hospital unit reserved for soldiers with emotional problems. The unit was surrounded by a barbed-wire fence, so the patients could not step outside and walk around. That they were caged in bothered me because throughout my childhood and adolescence, my siblings, friends, and I frequently engaged with the outdoors. For example, we ran or walked along the river, grew vegetables along the river, competed by swimming in the river, or threw stones in the river. Given these experiences, one day I started a conversation with the patients to explore how they experienced the unit and fence. A few patients responded that it made them feel "safe." Most responded that it made them feel "trapped like in a jail." I asked all of them if they wanted to take a walk. Those who felt "safe" declared "definitely not." The soldiers who felt trapped cheered. As we walked around the Army base, I noticed they became more relaxed, interactive, and they joked with each other. When we returned, one of the soldiers who elected not to take a walk wondered if anyone felt in danger. A soldier who had walked about replied with vigor, "Are you kidding; now I feel like a whole person!"

When I was hired to direct the Department of Child and Adolescent Psychology at McLean Hospital/Harvard University, I became very interested in including the outdoor environment for the inpatient population. Eventually I received permission from the director of the hospital to arrange aspects of the outdoors that the inpatient children and adolescents could engage when accompanied by staff (e.g., planting and caring for a vegetable garden; checking bird baths to see if they needed water; taking walks around the hospital grounds with a staff member). When I retired from McLean Hospital/Harvard Medical School the opportunity to explore the importance of the location in which psychotherapy is conducted, in addition to a playroom and office, became available. I established a nonprofit diagnostic-treatment center, and a donor made funds available to have a therapeutic garden constructed that included many features covering more than an acre of land. The various ways children and adolescents made use of this environment during psychotherapy sessions are described in detail (Santostefano, 2004).

My interest in the dialectical relationships among these concepts (i.e., embodied meanings, cognitive-emotional processes and behaviors used when negotiating with usual and unusual environments) was stimulated, for example, by an experience I had in a psychology class when an undergraduate at the University of Connecticut. The professor discussed an experiment that had been conducted within the discipline of Gestalt psychology, an experiment that amazed me. The investigators hung a banana from the ceiling of a cage, and placed a hungry monkey in it as well as a chair and a stick. The monkey raced about and leaped up to retrieve the banana, but could not reach it. Sometimes the monkey picked up the stick and leaped up, trying to knock down the banana, but still could not reach it. At other times the monkey moved the chair under the banana, jumped up on the chair, reached up, but still could not retrieve the banana. After many such efforts, the monkey apparently integrated the embodied meanings, related to these repeated physical activities, with the information his cognition and related emotions had gathered. With stick in hand, the monkey pushed the chair under the banana, jumped up on the chair, reached up and easily obtained the banana. My interest in the dialectical relations among meanings-emotions associated with body activity, cognitive processes, and behaviors used to negotiate goals continued to develop, resulting in my conducting studies that explored relations among actions, fantasies and verbal expressions (e.g., Santostefano, 1965b, 1977, 1985, and 1995).

Given the various experiences I share related to the origin of my interest in concepts detailed in the following chapters that guide when and why a therapist should initiate and participate in enactments, I was pleased when developmental research emphasized how meanings and related emotions are developed from body experiences in the first years of life (e.g., Sander, 1964, 1987; Stern, 1985). I was also pleased when the viewpoint of relational psychoanalysis emerged (e.g., Aron, 1996; Mitchel, 1988) emphasizing that sometimes when conducting psychotherapy, talking with adults, and talking with children while playing, is not enough. In addition and especially related to what is presented in the following chapters, relational psychoanalysis emphasizes that body experiences during the early years of life contribute throughout life to the meanings-emotions a person experiences and expresses (e.g., Aron and Anderson, 1998; Beebe and Lachman, 2014; Sletvold, 2014). Accordingly, relational psychoanalysis also emphasizes the importance of interaction, participation, negotiation, mutuality and enactment during psychotherapy. As Gabbard and Westen (2003) emphasize, "We no longer practice in an era in which interpretation is viewed as the exclusive therapeutic arrow in the analyst's quiver" (p. 203). I hope this volume contributes to the psychoanalytic-relational viewpoint by adding a therapeutic arrow in the analyst's quiver. Described in the following chapters, this arrow is designed to serve conducting therapy with children and adults whose embodied meanings, cognitive processes, and behaviors constantly interfere with their ability to experience, observe and reflect on themselves, to function adequately in everyday life, and to establish a growth fostering alliance with a therapist. In short, the mission of this volume is to demonstrate why engaging these adults and children in activities that enact particular embodied meanings serve to cultivate cognitive, emotional, and behavioral flexibility and provide a path that leads to the pathway of change.

Introduction

Bornstein (2001) noted that the field of psychoanalysis was facing an "impending death" and described "self-destructive behaviors by psychoanalysts that contributed to the decline of psychoanalytic theory" (p. 3). He noted, for example, that psychoanalysts focus on the contributions of early psychoanalytic practitioners and ignore the ideas and findings in other areas of psychology. He also pointed out that the exclusive use of several long-standing psychoanalytic techniques were of questionable value yet continued to dominate (e.g., free association, dream analysis). In response, he proposed that one way to save psychoanalysis is to donate "its organs to other subfields of psychology" (p. 12). In this volume I propose that another way to save relational-psychoanalytic psychotherapy is to donate organs from other subfields of psychology to relational psychoanalysis, in addition to donating the organs of psychoanalysis to other fields. Bornstein also recommended that to save psychoanalysis "psychoanalytic psychologists must make explicit the links between their concepts and findings and those of other disciplines in psychology" (p. 13). In response, another goal of this volume is to make explicit how a matrix of concepts described in chapter 1, and supported by research described in chapter 2, contributes to the viewpoint of relational psychoanalysis. This matrix of concepts includes the calls for action from usual and unusual environments and the calls for action from embodied meanings, both of which are perceived and managed by a person's cognitive-emotional orientation. If the person's cognitive-emotional orientation is focused either on the environment or on personal embodied meanings and emotions, the person responds with an instrumental-expressive behavior. That is, the person responds with an action or a fantasy or a verbal statement. This matrix also guides why and when a therapist should prescribe, initiate and participate in enactments with a patient who experienced trauma and major developmental interferences during childhood that produced rigid cognitive processes, emotions and behaviors. This rigidity prevents the patient from reflecting on his or her self and experiences, establishing a working alliance with the therapist, and benefiting from therapy.

The impending death of the general field of psychoanalysis was prevented, in my opinion, when the viewpoint of relational psychoanalysis emerged and gained momentum, launching a paradigm shift in psychoanalysis from drive theory to a relational model, focusing on patient-therapist interactions, and a paradigm shift from a one person psychology to a two person psychology (e.g., Aron, 1996). Years before relational psychoanalysis emerged, voices were heard that contributed to the launching of this paradigm shift. The following are examples. When Freud was cultivating his view that the analyst helps a patient transfer what is unconscious to the conscious level by expressing feelings and issues in words, Ferenczi and Rank (1924) published a book advocating that during psychoanalysis a range of experiences are expressed, recreated and enacted in the context of the patient-analyst relationship. Accordingly, they emphasized that the lived experience, either conscious or unconscious, is more important than expressing issues in words. Several decades later Harry Stack Sullivan (1953) proposed that psychoanalysis is the study of interpersonal relations and that the analyst, during a session, is both a participant and an observer. Along the same line, Hans Loewald (1960) emphasized that the process of change in analytic therapy is "set in motion not simply by the technical skill of the analyst, but by the fact that the analyst makes himself available for the development of a new 'object relationship' between the patient and analyst . . . " (pp. 224-225). Following these points of view, London (1964) proposed psychotherapy that integrates action and insight might be more effective, and also viewed the psychoanalytic process as a reactivation with the analyst of childhood interactions the patient had experienced with multiple environments. These positions opposed the dominant view of the time that the psychoanalyst should be a mirror, reflecting the patient's thoughts and emotions, and that the interpretation of transference and resistance is the only legitimate psychoanalytic technique.

The contributions by Donald W. Winnicott from the 1950s to 1970 are reviewed by Anderson (2014) who also provides summaries of interviews Anderson conducted with persons who had known Winnicott, or had been in analysis with him. He notes, for example, that one of Winnicott's major contributions to psychoanalytic theory "is his analysis of child development with an emphasis on the child's experiences early in life within the maternal matrix" (p. 376). Related to this issue, Winnicott also gave little emphasis to the importance of interpretation, a viewpoint expressed in the following comment Winnicott made that was provided by Rodman (1987), "The mothering technique is handed over to the analyst, and what I called the true self comes out of hiding . . . and risks living in a new environment I am able to provide . . . in the analytic setting" (p. 62). From this point of view, Winnicott also proposed the concept of creating a "holding environment" emphasizing that the therapist pay attention to what is going on, be present and supportive, take everything in and, if necessary, include physical contact. Patients have reported that sometimes Winnicott held their hand, and on one occasion when a patient cried, Winnicott put his hands out and asked the patient to cry in his hands.

More recently, voices can also be heard advocating the viewpoint of relational psychoanalysis. The following are examples. In his discussion of developments in psychoanalysis, Mitchell (1994) notes that the relational view is in sharp contrast to the classical view holding that while the therapist remains neutral, the "patient is expected to stop acting and instead speak about his conflictual feelings and thoughts" (p. 98). In what I view as an important elaboration of the issue Mitchell presents, Aron (1996) notes that relational psychoanalysis proposes, "The analyst influences the patient and the patient influences the analyst . . . the very essence of who the patient and analyst are with each other is negotiated" (p. 140). The relational influence of Hans Loewald on psychoanalytic theory and technique, noted above, is illustrated by Moscovitz (2014) who reports that from the 1960s to 2010 there has been a steady and sharp increase in the number of times Loewald's point of view has been cited in journals, namely his developmental model and analogies between the patient's interactions during childhood and analyst-patient interactions. Pine (1998) notes that since the mechanisms of change are always individualized according to the unique characteristics of the patient and analyst, it is not useful to view only a single mode of therapeutic action. In his comprehensive discussion of therapeutic action in psychoanalytic therapy Jones (2000) states, "The model of psychoanalytic therapy presented here emphasizes that there are two persons in the therapeutic relationship, and that the unconscious psychological processes of each influence the other" (p. xiv). And Toronto (2001) argues that, "As analysts have come to define the psychoanalytic field as a relational two-person enterprise, the role of the analyst has been redefined as a human one" (p. 38). Noted in the preface, Gabbard and Weston (2003) emphasize in their discussion of therapeutic action, "We no longer practice in an era in which interpretation is viewed as the exclusive therapeutic arrow in the analyst's quiver" (p. 823). They also elaborate on how psychoanalytic therapists now spend less time digging into the patient's past and instead focus on the ongoing interactions between the patient and therapist that provide information about how the patient's past experiences influence current conflicts the patient is experiencing. Along the same line, in a comprehensive discussion of Stephen Mitchell's view of interaction in psychoanalysis, Aron (2005) notes, " On one side are analysts who believe that there is a well-defined specific way to behave as an analyst, and that this behavior may be defined in terms of specific forms of technique, such as interpretation. On the other side are analysts who allow themselves the freedom to participate with greater flexibility and with an increased range of personal responsiveness" (p. 2–3). As a last example, a recent edited volume (Diamond & Christian, 2011) includes chapters that cover the history of psychoanalysis, from its initial focus on the importance of emotional conflict, fantasy, and insight to a paradigm shift that emphasizes, for example, the patient's relational experiences, interactions between the patient and analyst, and nonverbal processes in psychoanalysis.

From the viewpoint of these examples, I propose that rather than donating psychoanalytic organs to other subfields of psychology, the relational model has introduced organs from other fields of psychology into psychoanalysis. This results in a new understanding of the relationship between the body and mind, a person's internal world, the importance of interactions, and the dialectical process of change. Aron (1996) provides a comprehensive review of the emergence and history of the relational psychoanalytic viewpoint. Of the issues he addresses the following relate in particular to the focus of this volume: (1) "interaction itself is viewed as a factor that may legitimately lead to analytic change" because "interaction is itself interpretive, which is to say it conveys meaning" (p. 214); (2) Within "the relational model, unlike the classical one . . . enactments and reenactments are crucial therapeutic events that constitute the very essence of treatment" (p. 215); (3) "As the terms of interaction, enactment and actualization have become accepted . . . the Freudian community has undergone a conceptual and technical revolution" (p. 208); (4) "In interpersonal psychoanalytic work, the focus is on what the patient does with the analyst, how the patient is being with the analyst, rather predominantly on what the patient is saying to the analyst" (p. 75). What is presented in this volume includes this focus and also gives equal attention to the other side of the coin. Namely, it is also important to focus on what the therapist does with the patient, how the therapist is being with the patient, rather than what the therapist is saying to the patient.

The matrix of concepts presented in chapter 1 is intended to contribute to the mission of relational psychoanalysis. This matrix introduces and donates to relational psychoanalysis organs or concepts from developmental psychology, cognitive-emotional psychology, behavioral psychology, and environmental psychology. One concept addresses the embodied meanings, and related emotions, a person develops during the first years of life that form the foundation of a person's self. These embodied meanings and emotions interact with and influence three other processes. One process addresses how a person's cognition flexibly perceives and coordinates the information presented by an environment and the information expressed by a person's embodied meanings and emotions experienced in that particular environment. The second process addresses whether a person uses an action or a fantasy or a verbal statement when responding to a particular environment and responding to the embodied meanings and emotions experienced in that environment. The third process addresses how a person's cognition and behaviors manage environments that for the person are usual or unusual. Of special importance this matrix of concepts addresses how developmental interferences and traumatic experiences during childhood disrupt the flexible interaction among these processes and result in the person's cognition, behaviors, and emotions becoming very rigid. Because of this rigidity a person is not able to collaborate in relationships, develop a working alliance with a therapist, make growth fostering use of therapeutic experiences, and reflect on his or her thoughts and behaviors.

In chapter 2 I present a series of studies the results of which support the validity of the proposed matrix of concepts. For example studies explored the relation between a person's embodied meanings-emotions and the behaviors the person performs, the fantasies the person experiences, and the upsetting events the person discusses. Other studies explored how cognition regulates information and related emotions when a person negotiates and manages various environments such as preparing to perform a parachute jump while at an airport, anticipating surgery while in a hospital, and preparing for a final examination while in a college environment. In chapter 3 I describe psychotherapy I conducted with an adult, an adolescent and a child to illustrate why persons, who had developed very rigid cognitive-emotional processes and behaviors because of early developmental interferences, should be provided body experiences in psychotherapy consisting of a sequence of particular enactments with which the therapist participates.[1] The therapy cases illustrate that as these body experiences are repeated, the traumatic embodied meanings and emotions are experienced, modified, and eventually resolved. These enactments also promote cognitive, emotional, and behavioral flexibility that enables a person to establish a positive relationship and working alliance with a therapist and other persons. In chapter 4 I describe a psychodynamic-relational model of a sequence of enactments a therapist is urged to follow when a patient displays a rigid cognitive-emotional style, rigid behaviors, and is not able to benefit from discussing, free-associating, and analyzing thoughts and dreams. This sequence of enactments promotes a connection and interrelations among the parts of a patient's self that have been split and disconnected by traumatic experiences early in life.

I conclude this introduction with the following comments. In a previous publication (Santostefano, 2004) I discuss in detail the importance of enactments initiated and expressed by children during psychotherapy and why and how a therapist should participate in these enactments in order to revise the embodied meanings being expressed by the child. In this volume I propose, emphasize, and illustrate why with adult and adolescent clients, as well as with children, the therapist should prescribe, initiate, and participate in enactments. I recognize that the use of nonverbal, action-oriented techniques with children may seem appropriate to the therapist but appear "strange" if used with adolescents and adults. In response, it should be useful if I remind psychotherapists that as relational psychoanalysis gained momentum, attention was given to the use of nonverbal techniques with adults (e.g., Knoblauch, 1997; Wiener, 1999). In addition, the following statement by Aron (1996) is especially related to my thesis: "Interaction itself may legitimately lead to change" (p. 212).

NOTE

1. The names of patients and related persons were changed to protect anonymity.

ONE

A Matrix of Cognitive, Behavioral, and Environmental Processes that Enable a Patient to Function Adequately and Develop a Working Alliance with a Therapist

A Path to the Pathway of Change

When discussing the concept of transference in psychoanalytic therapy, Freud (1912–1958) proposed that the healthy part of the patient's ego enables the patient to develop a positive relationship with the therapist, and that this part of the relationship facilitates collaboration between patient and therapist as they work on the unhealthy parts of the patient's ego. Freud also proposed that if a part of the patient's ego is not healthy, analysis is not possible. During the following years, interest in this issue increased. For example, the term *ego alliance* was coined to conceptualize parts of the patient's ego that enabled the patient to collaborate with the therapist, a concept developed further as a *working alliance* (e.g., Greenson, 1965; Messer and Woltsky, 2010). In this chapter, I propose and describe a matrix of dialectically related processes from the fields of cognitive, behavioral and environmental psychology that are key aspects of a patient's self, and that enable the patient to develop a working alliance and collaborate with the therapist to resolve problems (figure 1.1). An important part of this proposal is that developmental interferences and traumatic experiences, occurring during the first years of a person's life, derail interrelationships among these processes, preventing a patient from constructing a working alliance with a therapist. When this occurs, the use of nonverbal interventions is emphasized to rehabilitate these processes, illustrated by therapy cases presented in chapter 4. The proposed matrix of interrelated, psychological processes relates to the conceptualization of a person's self to which we now turn.

We should pause at this point to note that the concept of self has become, "one of the hottest topics in psychology and psychotherapy" (Wolfe, 2003 p. 84). The concept of the self that William James (1890) proposed over a century ago is related to the matrix of psychological processes I propose. He noted that it is important to distinguish between two interrelated aspects of a person's sense of self, namely the "I-Self" and the "Me-Self," a concept that has had a major influence on the concept of the self (e.g., Harter, 1999). Aron (1998b) conceptualizes a dialectical relationship between the I-Self and the Me-Self, termed "self-reflexivity (the capacity to experience, observe and reflect on oneself as both subject and object)" (p. 3). This conceptualization relates in particular to the matrix of processes I describe in this chapter. Aron also proposes that in the absence of intense, emotionally upsetting experiences, the Me-Self continues to experience embodied meanings-emotions related to interactive-physical contact with persons and environments, and at the same time the I-Self perceives, interprets and gives meaning to these experiences and to what is going on.

At this point, I introduce the psychological processes of the proposed matrix, depicted in figure 1.1, that I propose play a significant role in the functioning of the Me-Self and I-Self. In general, the matrix conceptualizes the Me-Self as Embodied Meanings, forming the foundation or first floor of the self that symbolizes experiences beginning in the first years of life related to interactive-physical contact with persons and environments. These early experiences produce meanings and related emotions I term *embodied life metaphors* that continue throughout life influencing the meanings-emotions given to experiences. With further development two additional interrelated processes emerge that add to the formation of the self, depicted in figure 1.1 as the second floor: (1) Cognitive processes of the I-Self that perceive-register-interpret information-emotions related to the calls for action from environments with which a person is negotiating and, at the same time, that perceive and register the calls for action expressed by embodied meanings associated with environments being negotiated; (2) Nonverbal and verbal behaviors the I-Self uses to respond to the calls for action from environments and from related embodied meanings. The last concept of the proposed matrix relates to whether human and nonhuman environments with which a person is negotiating, and that express a call for action, are usual or unusual given a person's history, an issue related to environmental psychology. Concluding the introduction to this chapter, I remind the reader of the recommendation I made in the introduction; namely donating organs from subfields of psychology to psychoanalysis is one way to prevent the impending death the general field of psychoanalysis is facing, according to Bornstein

(2001). The matrix of concepts we now consider (supported by research presented in chapter 3) are organs from cognitive psychology, behavioral psychology, and environmental psychology. The proposed matrix of concepts also relates to the "integrated network of cognitive, affective, motivational and behavioral components or sub organizations of personality" presented by Beck (1996, p. 2) that contributed to the increase in attention the field of cognitive-behavioral therapy has received.

THE FIRST FLOOR AND FOUNDATION OF THE SELF: EMBODIED MEANINGS-LIFE METAPHORS

Body experiences and related emotions form the foundation of a person's self (e.g., Overton, Muller, and Newman, 2008; Santostefano, 1998b). It is important to consider a brief historical review of this issue and related methods, a topic detailed in a previous report (Santostefano, 2010). More

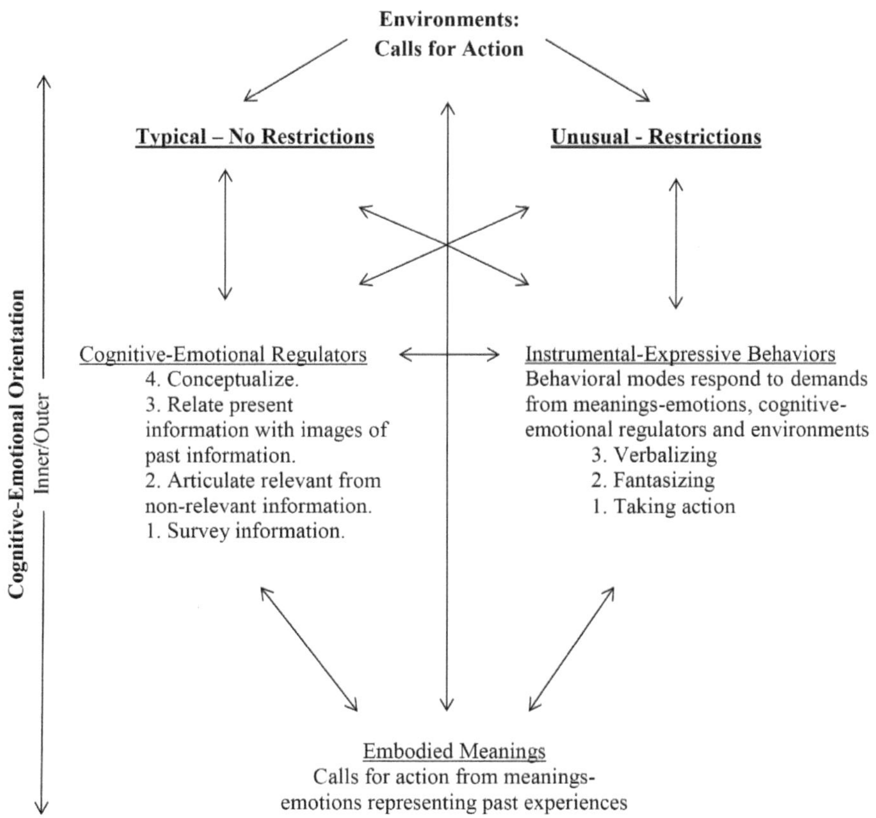

Figure 1.1.

than a century ago, before the concept of body image was introduced, Francis Galton (1884) devised a method to assess what could now be viewed as one aspect of the meanings-emotion a person's Me-Self experiences, and one aspect of the interpretation the I-Self gives to the experience. He noticed that persons who "have an inclination to one another . . . incline or slop together when sitting side by side" (p. 182). In an effort to explore the meaning of this behavior, he attached pressure gages to the legs of chairs located in a room where meetings were held. After each of several meetings, he recorded the measures to assess who leaned toward whom. Although he could not complete the experiment, he noted the importance of observing body activity that expressed meanings and emotions. Paul Shilder (1935) is credited with being the first to interrelate body experiences and personality with the concept of "body image," proposing that meanings are expressed by one's body and by clothing that is worn. Although he followed Freud who proposed that a "body ego" is constructed first forming the foundation of higher mental functions, he differed by emphasizing that a person's body image is a psychological process that continues to develop and change. Of particular relevance to the concept of embodied meanings proposed in what follows, Shilder also emphasized that the construction of a person's body image, and how it undergoes revisions, depends upon interactions and experiences the person has with human and nonhuman environments. Related to Galton's exploration of the meaning of the direction a person leans when seated, and to Shilder's conceptualization of body image, Fernald assessed "persistence" by recording the length of time a person stands on tiptoes (cited in Symonds, 1931), and Wolff (1943) observed how a child punched a balloon and manipulated a jar of cold cream to assess whether the child was expressing embodied meanings, such as aggression, insecurity and caution.

Years later several psychoanalysts addressed the concept of body image (Santostefano, 1998): for example, Carl Jung (1952) proposed that some persons, when coping with mental conflicts, experience their bodies as a protective enclosure to fend off attacks, and Theodore Rich (Freedman, 1977) proposed that some persons experience their bodies as an object with hard surfaces. Mahl (1987) also proposed a concept that relates in particular to this volume on the use of enactments. He noted that when a person repeats actions during a therapy session, the embodied meaning of the action is sometimes transformed into fantasies and conscious thoughts. For example, he described an adult patient who, during psychoanalytic treatment, repeatedly rubbed the back of her hand on a nearby, roughly plastered wall. Stimulated by these body experiences, a memory emerged. She described how her father regularly rubbed his beard against her face, a body experience that left her tingling with excitement. Related to this example, Wachtel (1987) emphasized the importance of studying the body language patients express during psychotherapy, and Kramer and Akhtar (1992) discussed how movements, gestures, postures, and other bodily expressions, that occur during psychoanalytic sessions, are a part of the patient's communications, expressing symbolic meanings.

From the viewpoint of this history, it is important to note that in the general field of psychology the definition of body image, and the methods used to assess body image, departed from the original position proposed by Shilder and pursued by psychoanalysts and other psychologists who conceptualize the body and mind as dialectically related (e.g., Overton, 2004). In contrast, a surge of research appeared in the general field of psychology conceptualizing body image as the manner in which a person construes her/his appearance, evaluated by questionaires and rating scales. For example, Thompson and Van der Berg (2002) describe eighteen assessment methods that ask participants to rate degree of satisfaction with underweight and overweight persons depicted by photos of male and female figures. This type of research, defining body image as satisfaction with appearance, has gained widespread interest illustrated, for example, by studies reported in a volume (Pruzinsky and Cash, 2002) that conceptualize body image in terms of how a person construes her/his appearance, and illustrated by a study that explored the influence the media has on satisfaction with one's appearance (Rogers, Sales, and Chabrol, 2010).

The conceptualization of body image as a person's view of her or his appearance evaluated with questionaires has been challenged. For example, one volume (Overton et. al., 2008) provides research that explores the role of body experiences in the development of meanings, cognitive processes and psychological functioning and emphasizes that body experiences produce multiple meanings rather than a singular "image" or "trait." In addition to this volume, and in contrast to body image research that focuses on the issue of appearance and the method of questionnaires, a few studies have used methods that stimulate a person's body to experience and express meanings. For example, Kring and Sloan (2007) assessed meanings conveyed by facial expressions. Tracy and Robins (2007) assessed meanings such as pride, fear, and disgust expressed, for example, by the direction of a person's eye gaze, posture, and arm position. To investigate fear of heights, Teachman and colleagues (2008) asked participants to climb a twelve-foot ladder and measured the time each participant took to ascend to the top. Related to these studies, Cash (2002) argued that researchers should discard the conceptualization of body image as body traits concerning appearance and, instead, assess "body image states in specific contexts or in response to environmental manipulation" (p. 164). Related to this proposal, at this point I discuss how a person's embodied meanings (i.e., body image) are constructed during the first years of life, when responding to specific contexts and environmental manipulation, and form the foundation and first floor of the self.

HOW EMBODIED MEANINGS ARE CONSTRUCTED DURING THE FIRST YEARS OF LIFE FORMING THE FOUNDATION OF THE SELF

Integrating the developmental research programs of Jean Piaget (e.g., 1951, 1967), Daniel Stern (1985) and Louis Sander (e.g., 1964, 1989) provides a perspective on how a matrix of embodied meanings and related emotions, representing interactive experiences, is constructed during the first years of life. Piaget's pioneering research demonstrated that infants construct knowledge and meanings while physically engaging and interacting with environments. His research was elaborated by Stern (1985) who focused on the emotions experienced during interpersonal interactions that contributed to the development of meanings. Stern also conceptualized that the meanings-emotions of repeated experiences with persons and things are conserved as representations of interactions that are generalized, a process he termed *RIG*. If activities and related emotions are repeated that differ in only minor ways, a generalized meaning is constructed that prescribes what to expect and how to perform. Whenever an experience occurs that is not similar to previously repeated experiences, a memory of the RIG is activated and serves to evaluate the ongoing experience. Piaget's and Stern's research is elaborated by Sander's (1989) that focused on a series of interpersonal issues child and caregiver "negotiate," contributing to the embodied meanings constructed. Because these embodied meanings represent both successes and failures of previous negotiations, Sander proposed that they influence how the infant seeks, engages or avoids future interactions with others and objects. Integrating these research programs defines the following stages in the development of the foundation of a person's self. This foundation consists of a constellation of embodied meanings and related emotions representing past experiences with persons and objects that prescribe how future persons and objects are experienced.

Emergent Self

From birth to three months, the self emerges as various body sensations are experienced when the infant contacts her/his body, the body of others and various objects in the environment. The infant repeats and elaborates these bodily sensations by engaging in activity that coordinates and integrates representations from different modalities (e.g., vision with touch, sound with touch) and from experiences with humans and objects. Piaget's observations of his two-month-old child provide an example (cited in Flavell, 1963, p. 93–94). The infant repeatedly and gently scratched his mother's bare shoulder during feeding time. When placed in a crib, he repeated another related cycle of behavior for about fifteen minutes. He scratched the bed sheet, held it for a moment, let it go, and then scratched it again. In addition, during these experiences initial adaption is negotiated as the infant enacts cues (e.g., various cries, sweeping arms back and forth, being content). Responding to these cues, the caregiver coordinates, for example, how the infant is held, fed, and bathed. If this phase is negotiated successfully, the infant develops, for example, a rhythm of sleeping and remaining awake, and the caregiver begins to develop a sense of "knowing" the baby.

Core Self

From four to seven months of age, the infant repeats behaviors to sustain contact with human and nonhuman environments, and negotiates reciprocal exchange. For example, the infant deliberately imitates a sound or movement performed by a person, so that this person will repeat the behavior and participate in a cycle of interactions. During these repeated interactions, the various activities, sensations and emotions experienced are integrated and conserved as representations of interactions that are generalized. In addition, during these interactions, caregiver and infant also negotiate reciprocating by taking turns being active and passive.

The development of the Core Self is illustrated by research conducted by Beebe and Lachman (2014) that addresses how attachment originates in face to face interactions between infant and mother. They individually invited a series of mothers and their four-month-old infants into the laboratory. Each mother was asked to play with her infant as she would at home, but without toys. Cameras were set to film the mother's face and hands, and the infant's face and hands, and filmed them for five to ten minutes. The films were microanalyzed with several scales (e.g., regarding the mother: whether or not she gazed at the infant's face, how closely she leaned toward the infant; regarding the infant: facial expressions, vocal expressions, orientation of the head, whether her/his skin or clothing or mother's skin or clothing was touched). The results document that mother-infant interaction is a continuous process during which they co-create their face-to-face communication and illustrate how, "processes of self-regulation and interactive regulation go on simultaneously within each partner. Each person monitors and coordinates with the partner, and at the same time regulates his or her own inner states" (p. 5). The results that emerge from the development of the Core Self make a significant contribute to the following phases of self-development.

Subjective Self

From eight to fourteen months the matrix of embodied meanings representing the circular reactions of the previous stages is elaborated as the infant continues interacting with human and nonhuman environments. The infant is now able to deal with new situations and imitate the actions of others with analogous behaviors. For example, when Piaget opened and closed his eyes, the infant first opened and closed his hand and then opened and closed his mouth. In addition during this phase the infant begins to use smiles and gestures to initiate and direct interactions. Also, since the toddler is physically more mobile, he/she sends more cues to caregivers that concern the need to explore the unknown and to be protected from stressful stimulation, while the toddler cultivates individuation.

Symbolic-Verbal Self

From fifteen to twenty-four months, the child develops the ability to negotiate self-assertion and aggression. Also, the toddler repeats behaviors to experiment with the environment, to symbolically represent objects, persons, and events, and to create play rituals. In addition, when an important person is absent, the toddler performs some action representing and conserving the meaning of that person. As one example, a twenty-month-old toddler was sitting in a high chair with a babysitter nearby and observed his mother place a hat on her head, say good-bye, and leave the room. The toddler placed a napkin on his head, expressing the meaning, "Although you're gone, you're still with me." Illustrated by this example, during this phase, the caregiver and toddler also begin to share meanings with symbolic verbal and action symbols they coauthor. Related to the example just cited, at mealtime this mother frequently "played a game." While preparing a meal, she playfully placed a napkin on the boy's head, "Wow, that's nice!" Sometimes, if she had not yet placed a napkin on his head, the boy would tap his head with the palm of his hand, laugh and exclaim, "Mama!" asking her to participate in the symbolic action they coauthored. Also in this developmental phase, as the toddler starts to walk, she/he cultivates the beginning of autonomy and shows the first signs of negativism. In response, the caregiver attempts to set limits or gives permission with both physical and emotional reactions. If this issue is successfully negotiated, the child experiences that some of her/his victories are being accepted and continues to negotiate and regulate self-assertion and aggression toward persons and things.

Narrative-Embodied Self Twenty-Five Months and Beyond

If the child and caregivers negotiated the previous issues with some success, they continue developing ways of communicating through symbolic behaviors (e.g., body postures, gestures, facial expressions) and continue to coauthor fantasy and verbal symbols during interactions. If this negotiating is successful, the child internalizes actions, emotions, meanings, fantasies, and verbal symbols that were shared, resulting in the construction of a matrix of embodied meanings that forms the foundation of the inner self and influences the meanings given to future experiences. I have conceptualized this matrix of embodied meanings as embodied life-metaphors "an organized constellation of bodily and touch sensations, actions, rhythms of gestures and dialogue, facial expressions, images, and emotions that represent past interactive experiences with human and nonhuman environments constructed while particular interactive/intrapersonal issues and needs are being negotiated . . . " (Santostefano, 2004, p. 35–36).

To illustrate how this foundation of embodied meanings-life metaphors influences future experiences consider the following example. At about twenty months of age, having adequately negotiated issues during the phases of the Emergent Self, Core Self, and Subjective Self, a child sat on his father's lap, directed him to button his shirt around the boy's body, and then directed him to unbutton his shirt. At this moment, the toddler quickly slipped off father's lap and ran away. The father responded by playfully searching for him behind furniture and in closets, laughing and shouting, "I know I'll find you!" During these playful interactions, this boy experienced and expressed the first edition of an embodied life-metaphor that represented negotiating attachment (at one with father's body) and separation-individuation (running off while father searched for him). Months later the child initiated another play ritual to continue negotiating this issue. At mealtime, whether at home or at a relative's house, sometimes he took a seat at the table next to his father, and sometimes sat at the opposite side of the table. By the age of three, he introduced another edition. At mealtime, he asked for a glass that was the same as his father's and that exactly the same amount of water be poured into each. The boy placed the glasses side by side and studied them, to ensure that each held the same amount of water. After he and his father each took a sip, the boy again placed the glasses side by side to judge which one had the "big" or "small" amount. Years later, based on the foundation of these embodied meanings-life-metaphors, the boy engaged father in playing the card game of "War" and still later, while maintaining a positive identification with father, engaged him in other games and in debates over the merits of various professional basketball teams. During high school, this boy became captain of three sports, performed well academically, and cultivated many friendships.

In addition to embodied meanings representing positive experiences with persons and environments, the foundation of the self could also contain embodied meanings representing traumatic experiences, an issue especially relevant to the process of psychodynamic psychotherapy. Related to this proposal, Beebe and Lachmann (2014) also incorporate the concepts of Piaget, Stern, and Sander, noted earlier, to emphasize the principal of developmental disruptions, namely that some interactions fail to satisfy what a child expects and needs from a caregiver. Addressing this issue, they emphasize that because the body is involved in everyday interactions between infant/toddler and caregiver, and because representations of these interactions influence how interactions are experienced throughout life, major disruptions that the infant/toddler experiences during these early negotiations influence how she/he experiences interactions throughout life, a viewpoint consistent with embodiment theory (e.g., Overton, Muller, and Newman, 2008). As one example of this issue, addressed in detail later, recall Piaget's observations of the two-month-old child who repeatedly and gently scratched his mother's bare shoulder during feeding time. What if this mother is obsessive and feels irritated when the infant scratches her shoulder. In response, the mother lays her hand over the infant's hand to interrupt and prevent the scratching. Such developmental interruptions during the first years of life would result in embodied meanings that influence how other persons and environments are experienced throughout life.

The following is an example of a major developmental disruption a young man experienced when a child, a disruption he revealed when participating in psychotherapy. Robert recently graduated from law school and was hired by a law firm. During therapy sessions he frequently discussed how he always felt very anxious and "on edge," whenever he was assigned a project. In addition, he always expected his supervisor to find something wrong and reprimand him for some reason. Robert also shared that his supervisor often pointed out that whenever he discussed a project with him, he noticed that Robert vigorously griped his hands together or squeezed the arms of the chair, and asked Robert why he was doing that. As Robert worked on this issue during several sessions, his associations produced the following, illustrating how embodied meanings representing a major developmental disruption influence current conflicts with others and environments. After Robert celebrated his second birthday, he apparently began negotiating self-assertion and individuation by playing a game he invented. While waving his arms, he ran from his bedroom to the top of a flight of stairs, abruptly stopped and burst out laughing. His parents, who happened to be nearby, pulled him back, slapped and scolded him, "You're not being careful! You might fall down the stairs." During these moments, he tried to express that he was playing "being a bird" and "flying like a bird," but the parents did not join his "game." For example, by running to the top of the stairs, laughing and waving their arms, they also could have pretended they were flying. Instead they refused to accept Robert's embodied metaphor. During therapy, because Robert was equipped with reflexivity, he eventually connected his linguistic metaphor of always "feeling on edge" when at work with his experiences at the top of the stairs and resolved his problem.

Related to these illustrations and to the concept that embodied meanings form the foundation of the self, Mark Johnson (2008) proposes that embodied meanings constructed during the first years of life are "metaphorically projected" into fantasies and verbal statements, influencing meanings a person gives to experiences throughout life, an issue studied and discussed by others (e.g., Overton, 1994; Santostefano, 1994; Brandstater, and Heckhausen cited in Poulin, Haase, and Heckman, 2005). Along the same line Benveniste (1998) discusses how linguistic metaphors derive from body experiences and proposes that many conventional statements demonstrate this concept (e.g., "This relationship is suffocating me," "I bit off more than I could chew").

At this point I propose that in the absence of traumatic experiences, embodied meanings constructed during childhood not only influence the meanings-emotions a person gives to experiences throughout life but also influence and are dialectically related to the development of the two other processes within the Self (i.e., [1] cognitive processes that perceive and gather information and related emotions; [2] behaviors a person uses to respond to persons and environments). This issue takes us to the second floor of the Self, depicted in figure 1.1. Here we note that the embodied foundation of the self contributes to the organization of cognitive-emotional processes and instrumental-expressive behaviors. If early major developmental interferences and traumatic experiences have occurred, the embodied meanings and emotions of these experiences are metaphorically projected into a person's actions, fantasies, verbal statements and cognitive-emotional regulators, and produce rigidity in each of these processes. This rigidity enables a person to avoid experiencing and interacting with others to prevent other traumatic experiences from occurring. As a result, this person also lacks reflexivity, the capacity to observe and reflect on oneself as both subject and object (Aron, 1998b). Whenever cognitive and behavioral processes are disrupted, derailed and become rigid, this issue has significant relevance for psychotherapy.

THE SECOND FLOOR OF THE SELF

We now enter the second floor of the self and discuss two dialectically related systems: (1) cognitive-emotional processes that perceive-register and interrelate the calls for action from environments and embodied meanings; and (2) behavioral processes that respond to the calls for action from embodied meanings and environments with which a person is negotiating. Before we consider each of these dialectically related systems, it is important to note the following history.

Similar to the divide that that was maintained between the body and the mind (see previous discussion), another dualistic boundary was established and maintained between cognition and emotion during the early decades of the twentieth century with the goal of preserving cognition as rational, protecting it from emotions viewed as irrational (Bruner, 1986). Another boundary was established between cognition and behavior by orthodox behaviorism, renouncing the mind and cognition and declaring that the only legitimate topic for psychological study was overt behavior (Bearison and Zimiles, 1986). John B. Watson, who is credited with launching behaviorism, made clear what behaviorism was splitting off and renouncing. He noted that psychology should be "The [science of behavior] . . . never to use the terms consciousness, mental states, mind . . . imagery . . . " (cited in Messer and Winoker, 1984 p. 64). Although the research of other investigators (e.g., Piaget, 1951, Werner, 1964, Bruner, 1951) reintroduced the forbidden mind, contributing to the emergence of a cognitive science (Gardner, 1985), Piagetian researchers and others studied cognition as a system separate from personality, viewed emotions as irrelevant and the mind engaged in "information processing." It is interesting that Piaget acknowledged that he seldom referred to emotional processes and stated, "Freud focused on emotion, I chose intelligence," (Decarie, 1978, p. 183). Piaget gave the reason for his choice. "I have always [preferred] . . . the study of normalcy and the workings of the intellect over the tricks of the unconscious" (p. 116). He also shared that his preference was due to the profound effect his mother's poor mental health had on him when he was a child

Although the pace of research investigating the relations among cognition, emotion, and behavior has become vigorous (Rottenberg and Gross, 2007), "The classic antinomy between thought and emotion continues to persist as one of the 'great divides' for self-regulation research" (Sokol and Muller, 2007, p. 401–402). For example, one area of research focuses on "basic emotions," conceptualized as separate from cognition, and another proposes that "cognitive emotional strategies should be studied in a conceptually pure way, separate from behavioral strategies" (Amone-P'Olak, Garnefski, and Kraai, 2007, p. 657). Opposing these divides other researchers, following a psychodynamic point of view, have illustrated why it is important to conceptualize and investigate interrelations among cognitive, emotional, and behavioral processes operating within a person's conscious and unconscious inner self, as the person interacts with environments to negotiate goals and development (e.g., Santostefano, 2010). At this point I introduce one part of the second floor of a person's self, namely how particular cognitive processes regulate information and related emotions while a person negotiates with environments.

Cognitive-Emotional Regulators

I begin with a brief historical review of the contribution psychoanalytic psychologists made to the issue of cognitive-emotional processes, a contribution that may not be familiar to many psychoanalysts. Also this early contribution influenced the methods I developed and research I conducted and reported in chapter 3. Decades ago, because mainstream cognitive psychology focused on "information processing," psychoanalytically oriented researchers conducted three conferences, launching a revolution that became known as the "New Look" in cognitive science because of its focus on interrelating cognition and personality (Blake and Ramsey, 1951). The first conference was held in 1948 emphasizing that psychology had done little to integrate perception with personality. As one example, two psychoanalytic psychologists, George Klein and Herbert Schlesinger reported studies that investigated what they termed *perceptual attitudes*, conceptualized as coordinating information from environments and from unconscious meanings and emotions located within "the personal world of the perceiver." For example in one study, they administered the following pretest to each participant. A series of words (e.g., red, yellow, blue, green, purple, brown) was printed in a color different than the meaning of the word (e.g., the word red was printed in yellow, blue, or green but never in red). The participant was asked to ignore the words and name the colors as rapidly as possible. After each participant completed the pretest, the participant was served a thirst-inducing meal, and then asked to scan a picture of an ice cream soda surrounded by numbers, and place dots on a sheet of gridded paper where they judged each number to be located. The thirsty participants who performed best on the pretest (i.e., cognitively subordinated the meaning of words as irrelevant while naming colors) were the most accurate in locating the dots. This result suggested that these participants successfully subordinated meanings-emotions evoked by the ice cream soda while judging the location of the numbers.

In 1949 a second conference was held (Blake and Ramsey, 1951) emphasizing several themes: e.g., Hilgard pointed out that the group was trying to discover how perception may be influenced by realities outside and by the realities within a person's self; Frenkl-Brunswick emphasized that the best way to assess the balance a person maintains between the realities outside and the realities within the self is to evaluate the person coping with environments; and Klein elaborated his concept of perceptual attitudes, adding that individuals consistently use particular cognitive processes to balance stimulation from external environments and internal-unconscious meanings-emotions, processes he labeled *cognitive controls*.

The third conference held in 1955 (Gruber, Hammond and Jesser, 1957) addressed three topics: (1) Cognition is a process at the center of a person's adaptations to environments; (2) The environments to which a person adapts are cognitive representations rather than actual things; and (3) Unconscious cognitive processes determine what pictures a person takes of ingredients in environments. The New Look approach continued into the 1970s but was eclipsed in the 1980s by a second revolution that shifted the focus back to "processing information" and ignoring emotion (Gardner, 1985). After examining the focus of this second revolution, and relating it to his participation in the first revolution, Bruner (1992) urged researchers to return to the emphasis of the New Look, and Holt (1964) informed psychoanalysts that cognition was emerging as a powerful point of view and urged them to consider how New Look concepts and research could be applied in their clinical work.

Following Bruner's (1992) recommendation that researchers return to the New Look, I developed concepts and methods and conducted studies (reviewed in chapter 3) that addressed two domains interrelating cognitive, emotional, and behavioral processes as a person copes with usual or unusual environments. One domain was influenced by Klein's method, as noted earlier. I developed tests to assess cognitive processes that regulate and coordinate information from environments with meanings and emotions located within the personal world of the perceiver. The second domain was influenced by Frenkl-Brunswich's emphasis, also noted earlier, that the best way to assess how a person's cognitive functioning is influenced by realities outside and by realities within a person's unconscious is to observe the person coping with environments. The following section describes particular cognitive processes that coordinate information and calls for action from environments and from meanings-emotions a person's inner self experiences when dealing with these calls for action. Examples of studies evaluating cognition as persons coped with environments are described in chapter 3 and relate to the view that "emotion regulation is a process dealing with a person-environment problem" (Campos, Frankl, and Camras, 2004, p. 391) and also to the multiple code theory of sub symbolic, symbolic imagery and symbolic verbal codes proposed by Bucci (2000).

Cognitive-Emotional Regulators

Following Klein's concept and methodology of "cognitive controls" based upon research with adults, I devised several procedures to assess different cognitive processes that account for how children, adolescents and adults gather and use information while regulating related emotions and negotiating environments (e.g., Santostefano, 1978, 1998). This program of research identified the following hierarchy of five processes, initially labeled "Cognitive Controls" (e.g., Santostefano, 1978, 1988) and later renamed "Cognitive-Emotional Regulators" (Santostefano, 2010).

(1) **Focal Attention**: The process with which cognition surveys and registers a field of information and related emotions.

(2) **Field Articulation**: The process with which cognition manages and regulates information and related emotions that are relevant or irrelevant to the task at hand.

(3) **Leveling-Sharpening**: The process with which cognition constructs an image of information-emotions, holds that image in the sub-

conscious-unconscious and relates it to perceptions of present stimulation.

(4) **Equivalence Range**: The process with which cognition categorizes information in terms of meanings and related emotions.

From the viewpoint of this model, a person's cognition does not march through one cognitive stage of development and then another. Rather, throughout development, a person surveys fields of information, focuses on what is construed as relevant, compares present stimulation, as construed, with subconscious-unconscious representations of related stimulation, and categorizes stimulation being experienced in terms of meanings-emotions. While one or another Cognitive-Emotional Regulator may dominate at a particular moment or phase of development, all processes operate simultaneously to regulate-coordinate information from environments and from personal meanings-emotions.

At this point a question is raised. What roles do embodied meanings and cognitive-emotional regulators play in adaptation, and how do they relate to behaviors a person uses to negotiate with environments? This question relates to the concept of Cognitive-Emotional Orientation and the concept of a hierarchy of Instrumental-Expressive Behaviors.

Cognitive-Emotional Orientation

Cognitive-Emotional Regulators respond to and achieve some degree of coordination between two "calls for action" (Sarason and Sarason, 1981). One call for action comes from molar environments (e.g., home, neighborhood, school, workplace, dentist office) and molecular environments (e.g., gestures, facial expressions, verbal requests), each environment requesting particular motoric, cognitive, and emotional responses. The other call for action comes from embodied meanings and related emotions that have roots in, and are associated with, past experiences with these molar and molecular environments with which a person is negotiating. Each of these calls for action require particular cognitive, emotional, and behavioral responses. Coordinating these two "calls for action" is referred to as *cognitive-emotional orientation* (Santostefano, 2010). In normal development, an individual's cognitive-emotional regulators become accommodated to the calls for action from information and related meanings-emotions unique to the person's usual environments. However, when the environment makes new demands that a person elects to address, or when the environment shifts to what is unusual for a person and restricts the degree to which the person can actively engage it, a cognitive-emotional regulator flexibly reorganizes, for a brief period of time, in one of two directions in the service of coping successfully: (1) to an "outer orientation" that focuses on and responds to the call for action from stimulation in the environment while subordinating-repressing the call for action from subconscious-unconscious embodied meanings-emotions evoked by the environment; or (2) to an "inner orientation" that focuses on and responds to the call for action from subconscious-unconscious embodied meanings-emotions being experienced, while subordinating the call for action from stimulation in the environment. Once a degree of coordination is achieved between these two calls for action (i.e., from the environment and from embodied meanings-emotions), a person responds with a physical action, or a fantasy, or verbalization. The concept of cognitive-emotional orientation contributes to Aron's (1998b) conceptualization of the dialectical relationship between the I-Self and Me-Self cited at the beginning of this chapter. The research studies described in chapter 3 will illustrate how the concept of cognitive-emotional orientation serves as a useful guide to evaluate whether a person flexibly shifts for a brief period of time from an inner to an outer cognitive orientation, or from an outer to an inner orientation, displaying reflexivity, that is associated with negotiating environments successfully. The therapy cases described in chapter 4 illustrate how traumatic experiences during childhood disrupt cognitive-emotional flexibility and the dialectical relationship between the I-Self and Me-Self. The therapy cases also illustrate how these developmental disruptions result in rigid meanings the Me-Self assigns to all interactions, and in the rigid interpretation and behaviors the I-Self prescribes when interacting with others and environments.

To illustrate reflexivity and a flexible cognitive-emotional orientation when it has not been derailed by developmental interferences, I return to the case of Robert. As noted earlier, Robert was a young lawyer who discussed from the start of his psychotherapy that he always felt very anxious and "on edge." During one session early in treatment, he quickly entered the office, sat down and exclaimed, "It happened again! It really got me nervous!" With a tone of concern and interest I asked, "What happened?" Engaged in an outer cognitive-emotional orientation, Robert looked directly at me and described in detail that his supervisor walked into the office holding a stack of paper. Then Robert shifted to an inner cognitive-emotional orientation, lowered his head, tightly gripped the arms of the chair, stared at the rug under his feet, took a deep breath, and then clutched the palms of his hand together. To explore the issue, I asked, "Robert, what else can you tell me about this?" In response Robert's cognitive-emotional orientation shifted back to an outer cognitive-emotional orientation, and he shared details; for example, his supervisor seemed to have an angry expression on his face and his eyes glared. To continue exploring, I asked, "Robert, does all of what you just shared remind you of anything?" Now Robert's cognition ignored the external environment and flexibly shifted to an inner orientation, scanning embodied meanings and related emotions. With much feeling, he recalled and relived another incident when the family was visiting relatives who lived in a rural area. Robert was eager to show his cousins that he can fly like a bird. Waving his arms and laughing, he ran across the road. His father spotted him, rushed over, scolded and slapped him. With a smile Robert added that this was one of the times that his uncle, his father's brother, disagreed and argued that he should not have scolded and slapped Robert. Robert added and emphasized that he always felt very attached and connected with this uncle because of the many positive, playful experiences they had together. At this point I expressed empathy, noted that he again shared another painful experience, and asked him to consider how experiences with his parents he shared could influence the way he experiences his supervisor. Stimulated by this interpretation, Robert experienced reflexivity, and his cognitive-emotional orientation flexibly shifted back and forth from an outer and inner position as he shared and related other experiences with his supervisor and his parents. Robert soon developed insight into how his past experiences with his parents shaped his painful experiences when interacting with his supervisor, and how past experiences with his uncle contributed to his having positive experiences with others.

With this example I illustrate that usually a person's cognitive-emotional orientation shifts flexibly, back and forth, from an outer to an inner position while interrelating past and present experiences and regulating the calls for action from environments and embodied meanings-emotions associated with past experiences. This brief example also illustrates how a flexible cognitive-emotional orientation contributes to the construction of insight and understanding. However, the focus of this volume is that some persons lack cognitive-emotional flexibility because they have experienced major trauma and developmental interferences. Such experiences disrupt reflexivity and result in one of the following maladaptive cognitive emotional orientations that interferes with a person establishing a working alliance with a therapist and benefitting from the process of psychotherapy: (1) a very rigid outer orientation: a person constantly focuses on stimuli in the environment and related emotions to avoid the participation of embodied meanings–emotions related to past traumatic experiences; (2) a very rigid inner orientation: a person constantly focuses on personal meanings-emotions to avoid the participation of stimulation from environments; (3) a very rigid outer or inner orientation when interacting with particular persons or issues.

Instrumental-Expressive Behaviors

A person responds to embodied meanings, to what his/her cognitive-emotional orientation perceives, and to what the environment is requesting by taking action, or engaging in a fantasy, or verbalizing. Each of these behavioral modes are conceptualized as containing two qualities that are equal: (1) an instrumental quality that serves to achieve a goal; and (2) an expressive quality that serves experiencing and expressing a personal meaning-emotion associated with the behavior and intended goal (Overton, 2006). It should be noted that from this viewpoint, the same instrumental quality could contain different expressive qualities. To illustrate this issue, consider a young girl walking along the beach, holding her father's hand. Suddenly, she stops, thrusts her arms upward, points at a bird and gasps. When the father asks the girl if she's OK, she replies, "That bird can really fly!" In this example, the instrumental quality portrayed by thrusting arms upward and gasping contains the expressive quality of pride and accomplishment. Consider another example of a young girl walking along the beach and holding her father's hand. Suddenly, this girl stops, pushes her arms upward, points at a bird and gasps. When this father asks his daughter if she's OK, she replies, "That bird can bite us!" With this example, the instrumental quality of pushing arms upward and gasping contains the expressive quality of fear and danger. We should also note that the same expressive quality could be contained in different instrumental behaviors. For example, the child who experienced the bird as dangerous also checks the front door every evening to make sure it is locked, and the child who experienced the bird as a powerful flyer frequently hangs her drawings on the wall of her bedroom with pride.

Before I introduce the proposed hierarchy of instrumental-expressive behaviors, it is important to pause and consider how this concept was considered. The history of the concept of instrumental-expressive behaviors relates to Galton who, as I noted earlier, examined the meaning expressed by the direction in which a person leans when seated with others. As another example, Hugh Hartshorne and Mark A. May (Symonds, 1931) studied "honesty" by presenting each participant with a sheet of cardboard on which were randomly printed ten circles of varying diameters. Each participant was asked to scan the circles printed on the cardboard, then close his eyes, and try to write a number in each circle, ranking the circles from the smallest to the largest; i.e., the number 1 in the smallest circle and the number 10 in the largest circle. Participants who located a correct number in some of the circles cheered and complimented themselves. For these participants the instrumental quality of being dishonest (i.e., keeping one's eyes closed and occasionally taking a peek at the board) was associated with the expressive quality of pride and pleasure. Participants who wrote numbers scattered over the board, failing to locate a correct number in a circle, also complimented themselves for their effort. For these participants the instrumental quality of being honest (i.e., keeping one's eyes closed) was associated with the expressive quality of pride and pleasure. Relying on their study of the relation between quality of writing and manner of speaking, Allport and Vernon (1933) coined the term *expressive movements*. Two decades later, R. B. Cattell (1957) assessed the degree to which the expressive quality of fright interferes with one's instrumental performance. He asked participants to complete a finger maze under two conditions: (1) with nothing surrounding the maze; and (2) with the maze surrounded by a cage containing a rat and cockroaches. Other investigators continued to explore the relationships among what a child expressed in fantasy (e.g., a story stimulated by a picture of the TAT), in language (e.g., responses to a questionnaire), and in action (e.g., behaviors displayed in the playground) (e.g., Crandall, 1963; Lindzey and Tejessy, 1956; Megargee, 1965; Rader, 1957). Related to these studies, Brown (1958) urged investigators to continue exploring the relationships between overt behavior and inner experiences.

However, since the 1980s interest in exploring relationships among modes of instrumental-expressive behaviors has declined. Illustrated by a comprehensive handbook (Hersen, 2003), the focus that has gained attention addresses two broad categories of methods to assess behavior, and what is broadly termed *personality*: "objective methods" (e.g., inventories; questionaires) and "projective methods" (e.g., the Rorschach Inkblot Test). Along the same line, a growing literature referred to as "trait psychology" proposes that behaviors fall within one of five basic traits that underlie personality (Costa and Widiger, 2001). The focus on traits and self-reports has been criticized by Kagan (2005). Reinicke and Freeman (2007) propose that an alternative solution "may be to adopt a dimensional approach" (p. 690), a view Piaget (1975) expressed decades ago when he recommended that investigators and clinicians consider psychological functioning in terms of the "ensemble of elements" (p. vii) involved as a person negotiates with environments to achieve some goal.

Stimulated by this issue, I developed methods and conducted studies (several are described in chapter 3) that support the following developmental hierarchy of instrumental-expressive behaviors (e.g., Santostefano, 1965b, 1968a, 1968b, 1970, 1985, 1998). Results indicate that taking action, fantasizing, and verbalizing are alternative modalities with which a person achieves some goal (instrumental quality), and at the same time symbolizes meanings (expressive quality). In addition, the results indicate that although the three modalities function throughout the life span, a developmental principle defines the relations among them as well as the modality that plays a major role during different phases of development.

(1) **Action Phase**: from about two to seven years of age, children tend to negotiate goals (instrumental quality) and experience-express meanings (expressive quality) primarily with actions, gestures, body postures, and facial expressions.

(2) **Fantasy Phase**: from about the ages of eight to eleven years, the action mode is subordinated and assimilated into the fantasy mode. In this phase, images and fantasies are the vehicles used most often to rehearse some action, before acutally taking action, to negotiate a goal (in-

strumental quality) and also to experience and express a meaning (expressive quality).

(3) **Language Phase**: From about the age of twelve years and beyond, the action and fantasy modes are subordinated and assimilated into the language mode that dominates.

The age when the use of each of these modalities begins is not exact but typically begins within the age range noted. Also each modality usually dominates until the next modality becomes dominant. A modality could become rigid so that, for example, a person could mostly use actions, or become lost in fantasies, during childhood and adolescence.

This model emphasizes several issues related to how direct or delayed a person is with the behavior he or she is using. First it is important to note that during adolescence and adulthood, although the action and fantasy modes are subordinated, they are not replaced but remain potentially active so that a person may shift from one to the other. In addition, when fantasizing a person distances himself from other persons and objects and delays taking action for the duration of the fantasy. Also, when verbalizing, the instrumental quality of this behavior is least direct and most delayed in terms of physical contact with persons and environments. Studies also illustrate that each modality is organized in terms of developmental levels from instrumental expressions that are most direct and immediate to instrumental expressions that are indirect and delayed. That action, fantasy, and language are available as alternative behavioral modes, and that each mode consists of a range of degrees of directness and delay, provides a person with multiple, alternative behavioral means to negotiate and achieve some goal (instrumental quality) and to express an embodied meaning (expressive quality). It should be useful to note that in one review of research (Stoops, 1974) fifty-five studies by other investigators who compared modes of expression (action, fantasy, language) support the model outlined above, although different assessment methods were used from those to be described in chapter 3.

In my opinion, one of the first "studies" illustrating the interrelations among actions, fantasies, and verbal expressions was described by Freud (Erikson, 1950). When Freud was living with a couple and their son, he noticed that the boy played a certain "game" many times. He repeatedly hurled various objects into the corner of his room or under his cot. Each time he hurled an object he made a sound that the parents and Freud understood meant "gone." Later, the boy introduced an edition to this behavior that involved a string wound around a wooden reel. Holding the string in one hand, the boy repeatedly hurled the reel with the other hand. Each time he hurled the reel he again made the sound, "gone," but now added a detail. Pulling on the string, he drew the reel back, and when the reel reached him, he made a sound meaning "there." Freud observed that later the toddler made the sounds "gone" and "there" when mother left the house and then returned. From the point of view of the model of instrumental-expressive behaviors, this boy demonstrated that the instrumental-expressive quality expressed in action behavior could be expressed in a fantasy, and then again in spoken words. Also from the viewpoint of this model, in normal development, the behavioral modalities of action, fantasy, and language are engaged in a dialectical process: i.e., each modality transfers its instrumental capacity and expressive qualities to the other modalities; in addition, each modality internalizes, and is influenced by, the instrumental and expressive qualities of the other modalities.

Maladaptive Instrumental-Expressive Behaviors

Significant traumatic, developmental disruptions that occurred during childhood, and have not been repaired, not only comprise a person's cognitive-emotional orientation (noted earlier) but also the dialectical relations among the modalities of action, fantasy, and language as tools used to negotiate goals (instrumental quality of behavior), and to experience-express embodied meanings associated with the negotiating (expressive quality of behavior). Major disruptions result in one of the behavioral modalities (i.e., either action, fantasy, or language) becoming rigidly dominant and segregated from the others, a system of instrumental-expressive behaviors that continues operating into adulthood. Accordingly, when a person who experienced major developmental disruptions negotiates goals while interacting, fantasies do not adequately serve as instrumental-expressive behaviors temporarily substituting for actions, and verbal statements do not serve as instrumental-expressive behaviors temporarily substituting for actions and fantasies. The cases presented in chapter 3 contain vivid examples of rigid instrumental-expressive behaviors displayed by a child, an adolescent, and an adult.

The following two sketches provide brief illustrations of this issue. When he was five years old, a boy was standing at the edge of a field watching his father operate a tractor. Suddenly the tractor tipped over, and his father was crushed to death. This boy had been very attached to his father; for example, they often engaged in games, they gardened, and the boy always enjoyed watching his father operate the tractor. Before this tragedy, the boy's interactive style had been exuberant and interactive. Now he became very withdrawn and inhibited, and his mother also became very depressed. This boy was referred for a psychological evaluation and treatment because the teachers at his school had become concerned. In contrast to his previous relational style, they observed that he had become "like a zombie." For example, he failed to respond when his teacher tried to interact with him, and during recess he stood at the edge of the playground, failing to respond to classmates. In terms of the models outlined, the trauma experienced by this boy related to his father's tragic death not only resulted in a rigid inner cognitive-emotional orientation but also in his fantasy mode becoming very rigid and dominant, blocking the availability of the action and language modes to negotiate with persons and environments.

The second illustration concerns a high-school student, John. During my first session with him, when I asked how I could be of help, he leaned forward, pushed aside his wavy hair and revealed an area more than one inch square that was bald. He shared that every day, when he prepares to go to school, he carefully feels the bald area with his fingertips. If he detects a hair stub, he plucks it out and feels a surge of pleasure. He also shared that he has been pulling hair from that area of his head ever since he was a child. He then associated to an issue he declared was the reason he requested a consultation. With difficulty, he described the surge of anger and excitement he experiences when interacting with a teacher who maintains a beard. With John's permission I met with his parents who shared that, although John's hair pulling was of some concern, they were more worried about his poor academic performance. Influenced by my meeting with John, at one point I asked father if he ever maintained a beard. Although he was surprised by my question, he acknowledged that years ago he did have a beard. He also shared that he enjoyed snuggling his beard on John's belly and neck from the time John was a baby until he started kindergarten. With amusement the father added that when John began to walk, sometimes John would walk by him, arch his back and push out his belly, inviting father to tickle him. At one point in this discussion, John's mother asked her husband to recall what happened when he shaved his beard. Father shared that John seemed stressed and elaborated that for reasons he does not understand, after he shaved his beard he stopped playing games with John. In terms of the model we are considering, John experienced a major developmental disruption and interference, namely excessive, inappropriate stimulation from his father's beard that was suddenly interrupted, as was father's playfulness. Accordingly, the action mode (hair pulling from childhood to adolescence) became rigid and dominated, preventing participation from the fantasy and verbal modes, as John continued developing and interacting.

Before leaving the second floor of the self, we should note that traumatic experiences not only disrupt the development and dialectical relationships among cognitive-emotional regulators, and the development and dialectical relationships among instrumental-expressive behaviors, but also damage the hallway that connects and allows interaction among cognitive, emotional, and behavioral processes. This issue is illustrated by the therapy cases to be presented in chapter 4.

THE THIRD FLOOR OF THE SELF: USUAL AND UNUSUAL ENVIRONMENTS THAT CALL FOR ACTION

We now enter the third floor of the self, depicted in figure 1.1. Here we address the relations between the calls for action from environments and from embodied meanings that are processed and regulated by a person's cognitive-emotional regulators, to which a person responds with instrumental-expressive behaviors. At the start, it is important to note that the concept of environment has been addressed with two metatheories, each providing a different definition of the environment as it relates to psychological development and functioning. Accordingly, these alternative conceptualizations are briefly reviewed to ensure the clarity of the conceptualization of environments that I propose.

The Viewpoint of the Environment Advocated by Behaviorism, Environmental Psychology, and Ecopsychology

The first conceptualization of the environment emerged in the 1920s and shaped the model of behaviorism. This viewpoint erected a boundary between a person and environment, defining the environment as a context that delivers stimulation-information independent of a person to which the person responds. Accordingly, this concept viewed the environment as an independent source that activates a person to respond. B. F. Skinner (1974) elaborated this concept by introducing his principle of "operant learning," and the "ABC" of behavioral theory. "A" is the environmental condition that evokes a person to produce some form of behavior "B," which produces some consequence "C" in the environment. The environment responds with a reward, so that the behavior is maintained and repeated, or responds with a punishment so that the behavior is eliminated. Hollin (1990) applied this viewpoint to assess young offenders and noted, "[since] the consequences of an individual's behavior are delivered by the environment in which the behavior occurs, then the cause or determinants of behavior are to be found outside the person" (p. 8).

This dualistic model of behaviorism contributed to the foundation of environmental psychology and ecopsychology. Environmental psychology focused on constructing an understanding of how environments determine behaviors (e.g., Bonauito and Bonnes, 2000). For example, Sako (1977) compared the behavior of children attending small schools with the behavior of children attending large schools and reported that small schools stimulate children to participate more responsibly. Following the same viewpoint, ecopsychology focused on the concept that some environments contain stimulation-ingredients that automatically have a positive influence on a person. Several studies advocating this position are reviewed and cited (Santostefano, 2004). For example, adults who walked through an area filled with trees and vegetation were more relaxed than adults who walked through an urban area. Adults sitting in a waiting room of a dental clinic were less stressed when a large mural, depicting mountains and trees, was hung on the wall than were adults who sat in the same waiting room when the wall was blank. As another illustration, university students who were experiencing mild stress because of a final exam recovered to a greater degree after viewing slides of rural settings than did students who viewed slides of urban settings. That the momentum of this viewpoint increased is illustrated by newspaper articles informing readers that flowers and gardening can improve a person's mental health (e.g., Waldholz, 2003).

The Viewpoint of the Environment Advocated by Relational-Developmental Psychology

One contribution to the roots of this viewpoint came from the psychoanalyst Heinz Hartmann (1939/1958) who introduced the concepts of "autoplasticity" and "alloplasticity" to conceptualize dialectical-reciprocal relations between a person and environments; namely the person changes an environment or the environment changes a person. He also emphasized the importance of conceptualizing whether environmental stimulation is usual or unusual given a person's history. This viewpoint was followed by the model of "transactionalism" (Wapner and Demick, 2000) that conceptualizes a person and environment forming an holistic organization and emphasizes that a change in any part of the system affects the whole system. The model of transactionalism also proposes that a body-self experience with the environment does not replace earlier experiences but integrates them, a view converging with embodiment theory (Overton, Muller and Newman, 2008). In addition, this viewpoint emphasizes that a person interprets environments according to personal intentions and behaves accordingly. As one example, this model was used in one study (Wapner and Demick, 2000) to examine differences in behavior that hospitalized psychiatric patients displayed before and after the entire community was relocated.

The conceptualization of the environment held by relational-developmental psychology has been elaborated and supported by investigations (Bronfenbrenner and Morris, 2008). This model stresses that it is important to observe a person interacting with different aspects of the environment and assess the relational, bidirectional interactions among psychological processes involved as a person negotiates with an environment. Two particular processes are emphasized: (1) the instrumental-expressive behaviors a person typically uses when engaging and interacting with human and nonhuman environments; and (2) the unique cognitive, emotional, and behavioral characteristics of a person. This point of view also emphasizes that the environment is not only considered in terms of its objective-physical makeup, but also in terms of how the ingredients of the environment are subjectively experienced. Related to the viewpoint that I advocate, Good (2007) provides an historical review of the "skirmishes" that have taken place regarding the relations between persons and environments. Good also reviews studies illustrating why it is important to note whether an environment provides a person the opportunity to take some action that serves achieving a goal or limits/inhibits a person from taking some action to achieve a goal. This issue is illustrated by studies I conducted and describe in chapter 3; for example, the cognitive-emotional functioning of participants assessed when in a hospital anticipating surgery and the cognitive-emotional functioning of participants assessed when at an airport about to perform a parachute jump. Good also stresses that "mind, body and environment cannot be understood in isolation, but are constructions from the flow of purposive activity in the world" (p. 269).

CONCLUDING COMMENT

The utility and significance of the matrix of interrelated processes that I describe in this chapter (embodied meanings, cognitive-emotional regulators, instrumental-expressive behaviors, and environments) are illustrated by the studies presented in the next chapter. In addition, the utility and significance of this matrix is illustrated when the concepts are used as a guide to conduct psychotherapy with adults and children who participate in all environments using the same, rigid inner or outer cognitive-emotional orientation and the same rigid instrumental-expressive behavior that developed to avoid embodied meanings related to early traumatic experiences. When conducting psychotherapy with these patients, illustrated by the cases presented in chapter 4, therapy should begin by focusing on, and engaging, the first floor of the patient's self with particular enactments. Repeating these enactments cultivates flexibility in the patient's cognitive-emotional orientation and in the patient's instrumental-expressive behaviors, revising the second floor of the patient's self. Once reflexivity is developed, the patient resolves meanings related to past traumatic experiences and engages and responds to all environments more flexibly and successfully.

TWO

Studies Investigating Dialectical Relations among Embodied Meanings, Cognitive-Emotional Regulators, Instrumental-Expressive Behaviors, and Environments

The studies reviewed in this chapter make clear the links between the concepts and findings presented in the prior chapter and the conceptualizations and results from other subfields of psychology. In general, the studies reviewed explored the following issues: (A) dialectical relations between embodied meanings and meanings expressed in fantasies and conscious fears; (B) dialectical relations between embodied meanings and cognitive-emotional orientations; (C) dialectical relations between cognitive-emotional orientations and instrumental-expressive behaviors; and (D) dialectical relations between cognitive emotional orientations and instrumental-expressive behaviors when persons cope with and negotiate usual and unusual environments. The studies reviewed in what follows, in addition to other related studies, are reported in more detail in other publications (e.g., Santostefano, 1998, 2010, 2014).

DIALECTICAL RELATIONS BETWEEN EMBODIED MEANINGS AND MEANINGS EXPRESSED WITH FANTASIES

These studies compare embodied meanings expressed by a normal, high-school population, and by adolescents hospitalized in a psychiatric facility, with meanings these participants expressed when using the instrumental-expressive fantasy mode to describe fantasies stimulated by ink blots.

Methods

The Action Test of Body Image (ATBI)

As noted in chapter 2, the original conceptualization of body image, initiated by Paul Shilder and pursued by psychoanalysts, defined body image as the meanings-emotions expressed by a person's body activity. I also noted that this concept has been subordinated by research that conceptualizes body image as a person's opinion about his/her appearance, usually assessed with questionaires, a concept that has been challenged. Related to this issue, Thompson and van der Berg (2002) emphasize that, "Behavioral measures have received limited analysis in body image literature" (p. 150), and Yanover and Thompson (2009) note, "Researchers are still seeking a valid behavioral measure of body image for all age groups . . . " (p. 190).

Related to this issue and influenced by my experiences with the Miniature Situations Method discussed in the Preface, I designed the Action Test of Body Image (ATBI) to help a person's body speak and express meanings-emotions. (Santostefano, 1992, 1998b, 2010, 2015). With the ATBI a participant is asked to assume different body postures and perform various actions-gestures and, while engaging each body experience, describe thoughts, feelings, and meanings that come to mind. Some items ask the participant to engage his/her whole body (Macro Body Items), and other items ask the participant to engage parts of his/her body (Micro Body Items). The following are examples of Macro Body Items: (1) Lean against the wall; (2) Stretch and hold your arms out to the side; (3) Stand, spread your legs apart and encircle your arms toward your chest several times; (4) Stand on one leg, left your other leg, lean forward, and spread your arms out. Some examples of Micro Body Items are: (1) Open and close your eyes several times; (2) Pass the palm of your hand over this piece of fur; (3) Place your hand in this box without knowing what is in there; (4) Water this plant; (5) Twist this coat hanger.

Responses are evaluated with several scales. One set of scales rate a meaning-emotion on a 6-point scale; e.g., (A) The embodied meaning of imbalance-balance: 1 = "I feel like I'm falling off a cliff;" 6 = "I feel like I'm a ballet dancer." (B) The embodied meaning of constriction-assertion: 1 = "It makes me feel like I'm handcuffed;" 6 = "I feel like I'm running the marathon." Another set of scales evaluate whether particular embodied meanings are expressed (Score = 1) or not expressed (Score = 0); e.g., (A) Affiliation toward the self: "Reminds me how my friend hugged me;" "Like I'm hanging out with friends." (B) Aggression toward others: "This is the way I feel when I want to punch this guy." (C) Aggression toward the self: "Makes me feel like I'm getting shot." (D) Competence: "Makes me feel like I can do anything." (E) Incompetence: "Everyone could lift this steel bar but I couldn't." (F) Deformed/Inadequate: "Makes me think of a crippled guy I saw in a wheel chair." (G) Dependency: "Reminds me of holding onto a railing." (H) Unsafe/Danger: "Leaning over the edge of a building;" "Like I'm about to be hit by a car."

The Fantasy Interaction-Motion Scale (FIMS)

In contrast to scoring systems that focus on structured determinants of images constructed by participants when examining and associating to the Rorschach Inkblot Test, the FIMS scoring system I developed focuses on evaluating interactions-activities and related emotions expressed by images-fantasies, and also focuses on the integrity of humans, animals, and objects involved in the interactions-activities depicted. The validity of this scoring system has been supported by studies (e.g., Santostefano, 2015). Interactions depicted in Rorschach responses are rated by several scales. For example: (A) Developmental level of the interaction (9-point scale): 1 = self-interacting with itself (e.g., "A dog looking at its paw"); 9 = self-interacting with another self (e.g., "Two people dancing together"); (B) Level of vigor represented by the interaction-motion (6 point scale): 1 = extremely vigorous (e.g., "Looks like a tornado whirling over this house"); 6 = "This is a leaf floating down into her hands." Other scales rate the presence or absence of an attribute. For example, (C) Deformed agent or recipient involved in an interaction; (e.g., "This is a guy with three legs and a thing sticking out or his nose, and he's chasing this dog"); (D) Disintegration; (e.g., "This looks like a tunnel that's caving in").

Study I

The participants, fifty-five white adolescents (twenty-eight females; twenty-seven males; mean age of fifteen years) attending an inner-city high school were individually administered, with parental permission, the ATBI and the Rorschach Inkblot Test in school during a school day.

Results

No differences were observed associated with age or gender. A factor analysis was conducted with ATBI and FIMS scores to explore relations between meanings-emotions expressed when the body is the source of stimulation and when inkblots stimulate fantasies symbolizing unconscious meanings. The following are examples of results: (A) experiencing and expressing embodied meanings of assertion was associated with producing a high percentage of fantasies that depicted interactions; (B) experiencing and expressing the body-self as deformed, and lacking a sense of value, correlated with expressing fantasies that depicted interactions between incomplete persons and animals; (C) expressing embodied meanings of aggression and assertion correlated with expressing fantasies depicting vigorous interactions-motions.

Study II

The participants were seventy-eight children and adolescents (thirty-eight females; forty males; mean age of fifteen years) who had been admitted to an inpatient psychiatric facility because of various major psychological difficulties. On admission each participant was individually administered the ATBI and the Rorschach Inkblot test. A factor analysis was conducted with ATBI and FIMS scores to explore the relations between embodied meanings-emotions and fantasized meanings-emotions this hospitalized population produced. The following are examples: (A) Experiencing-expressing embodied meanings of fatigue correlated with fantasizing animals and objects involved in interactions, rather than humans; (B) Experiencing and expressing the body-self as deformed correlated with the absence of fantasizing disintegrated-modified agents and recipients engaged in interactions; (C) Experiencing and expressing embodied meanings of aggression toward others correlated with fantasizing interactions as occurring in slow motion.

Discussion

In general, the results of Study I (normal high-school group) suggest that a boundary does not exist between meanings-emotions stimulated by body activity and unconscious meanings-emotions stimulated by inkblots and expressed in fantasies, and that the modalities of body image and fantasy are concordant. In contrast, the results of Study II (hospitalized adolescent group) suggest that a boundary exists between meanings-emotions stimulated by body activity and meanings-emotions expressed in fantasies, and that the body-self modality and fantasy modality are not concordant. These results relate to the issue noted in chapters 1 and 2; namely that trauma and developmental interferences disrupt and segregate the dialectical interactions among the modalities of body image, cognitive-emotional regulators, and instrumental-expressive behaviors. From this viewpoint, the results of Study II illustrate that the fantasy mode of this inpatient population is not serving as an alternative modality to express, rehearse and negotiate meanings-emotions that are experienced at the body-self level. For example, the fantasy mode of this population did not fantasize humans performing interactions, instead of animals and objects, to negotiate and revise the embodied meaning of fatigue. As another example, experiencing the body-self as deformed was associated with the absence of fantasizing interactions among persons, animal and objects that are disintegrated in some way. Accordingly the embodied meaning of a deformed self is not being negotiated and revised by fantasizing interactions between persons and animals that are deformed in some way.

DIALECTICAL RELATIONS BETWEEN EMBODIED MEANINGS AND DISCUSSING STRESSFUL EVENTS

The second probe explores the relations between meanings-emotions stimulated by body activity and meanings-emotions expressed by stressful events a person elects to discuss.

Method

In addition to the ATBI (described in Probe I), the Life Stressor Interview (LSI) was developed, and used in the next two studies, to assess meanings-emotions expressed by events a person defines and discusses as having been stressful.

Life Stressor Interview

After the examiner and participant establish sufficient rapport, the examiner shares with the participant that everyone witnesses, or hears about something, that happened that is upsetting. Then the examiner comments, "I would like to ask you whether anything happened that you saw or heard about that upset you a lot." The examiner joins the participant in discussing the event reported, provides empathic support as indicated, and does not guide the participant's discussion in any direction. If the participant spontaneously describes one upsetting event, the examiner asks only once, "Is there anything else that upset you a lot?" Responses are scored in terms of types of stressful events described. For example: (A) global events (e.g., war, terrorism, social crises); (B) aggressive events; (C) harm to loved ones; (D) disruption in family relationships; (E) natural disaster.

Study III

The participants were ninety-three kindergarten children attending an inner-city school serving a blue collar socioeconomic population: thirty-nine females, fifty-four males; thirty-seven African Americans; fifty-one Latin Americans, four Whites, one Asian. All children were individually administered the ATBI and the LSI during a school day as part of an early detection program. ATBI responses of these children were correlated with the stressful events they discussed.

Results

The following are examples of the significant correlations obtained: (A) Children who experienced-expressed embodied meanings representing the body-self as deformed/inadequate also discussed stressful events involving shootings and fights; (B) children who experienced-expressed embodied meanings of danger discussed illness/hospitalization of a loved one; (C) Children who experienced-expressed embodied meanings of constriction, discussed the death of a loved one as stressful. In general these results illustrate concordance between the modalities of embodied meanings and the instrumental-expressive behavior of discussing stressful events. Another finding is noted because it could stimulate further study concerning the relation between the calls for action from environments and embodied meanings. Latin American children and African American children were compared because only four White children and one Asian child participated. During the ATBI, African American children experienced-expressed a significantly higher percentage of embodied meanings-emotions representing the body self as inadequate-deformed than did Latin American children. In addition, African American children discussed significantly more stressful events in response to the LSI than Latin American children.

Study IV

The participants were sixty-three white eleventh-grade students (thirty-six females; twenty-seven males) attending a public school that served a middle-class community located several miles from a large city. With parental permission, all students volunteered to participate and were individually administered the ATBI and LSI at school during a school day.

Results

Because no significant gender differences were observed in terms of types of stressful events discussed, and because almost half of the females and half of the males did not discuss at least one event, participants were combined to form two groups for statistical analyses: (1) Stressor Group: thirty-eight participants who discussed one or more stressful events; (2) Non-Stressor Group: twenty-five participants who did not discuss a stressful event. The following significant differences were obtained. Compared to participants who did not discuss any upsetting events, participants who discussed upsetting events experienced-expressed, in response to the ATBI, more meanings-emotions representing the body self as unsafe, as constricted and in need of affiliation.

Discussion

These studies illustrate that in normal development the modalities of experiencing-expressing embodied meanings and the modality of verbalizing-discussing events that express meanings-emotions are interrelated and concordant. For example, kindergarten children who discussed upsetting events involving shootings and fights, compared to those who did not, expressed meanings-emotions representing the body self as in danger; similarly adolescents who spontaneously discussed upsetting events, compared to those who did not, expressed meanings-emotions representing the body as unsafe. In general, the results obtained with these normal children and adolescents suggest that what the body says is also being expressed and negotiated in the instrumental-expressive verbal mode by discussing events representing related meanings-emotions. These results, produced by normal populations, indicate that if developmental interferences have not occurred, the embodied self and the instrumental-expressive verbal mode serve as alternative "theaters" where meanings-emotions are rehearsed and expressed.

DIALECTICAL RELATIONS BETWEEN EMBODIED MEANINGS AND THE ORIENTATION OF A COGNITIVE-EMOTIONAL REGULATOR

The following studies explored relations between embodied meanings-emotions experienced-expressed and the orientation of a cognitive emotional regulator that participants displayed.

Method

Of the cognitive emotional regulators described in chapter 2, the Leveling-Sharpening Regulator was evaluated in the studies of this probe. As noted in the previous chapter, the leveling-sharpening cognitive-emotional regulator is defined by the manner in which a person's cognition constructs an image of information and related emotions, holds that image in memory over time, and compares it to perceptions of stimulation that is present. Two tests were constructed for this study to evaluate the Leveling-Sharpening Regulator: The Leveling-Sharpening Shoot-Out Test (LSSOT) and The Leveling-Sharpening Friends Test (LSFT). Each test is identical in makeup, procedure, and task requirement. With each test sixty-three pictures of a scene (8 x 11 inches) are displayed in succession, five seconds each display. The participant is asked to scan each picture displayed and report any changes that occur in the scene she/he notices. Gradually throughout the series of sixty-three pictures that are displayed, twenty details are omitted as follows. The first three cards contain all the elements of the scene. Then on Card 4 a very small detail is omitted and remains absent from each of the remaining scenes. From this point on, a detail is omitted every three cards, each detail slightly larger, and more obvious, than the previous one, resulting in the omission of twenty details from the scene.

Two scenes were used to stimulate meanings-emotions that a participant is required to regulate as she/he copes with the cognitive task of holding the details of the scene in memory and noticing whether any changes occur. The LSSOT for male participants consisted of a scene of two cowboys in a shootout and for females two cowgirls in a shoot-out. The LSFT for males consisted of a scene of two cowboys smiling and greeting each other and for females two cowgirls smiling and greeting each other. Performance with each test was evaluated with two scores: (1) the number of correct changes detected; (2) how soon a change is perceived once it is introduced. The sooner the first change is perceived, the greater the number of changes detected, and the sooner a change is perceived once it is introduced is termed *cognitive sharpening*, reflecting an outer Cognitive-Emotional Orientation that focuses on ingredients in the scene while subordinating meanings-emotions evoked by the scene. The later the first change is perceived, the fewer the number of correct changes perceived, and the greater the lag before a change is detected is termed *cognitive leveling*, reflecting an inner Cognitive-Emotional Orientation that focuses on personal meanings-emotions stimulated by the scene while subordinating details of the scene.

Study V

Participants were ninety-three children attending a public-school kindergarten class who did not present learning or adjustment problems (thirty-nine females; fifty-four males). With parental permission each child was administered the following procedures at school during a school day: the ATBI, the LSSOT, and the LSFT.

Results

Children who experienced-expressed embodied meanings-emotions of balance detected more correct changes and sooner (outer cognitive-emotional orientation) with both the LSFT and the LSSOT. In contrast children who experienced-expressed body imbalance perceived fewer changes and later (inner cognitive-emotional orientation) with both procedures. Other results showed relationships between the expression of particular embodied meanings-emotions and the cognitive-emotional orientation assumed when responding to the LSSOT versus the LSFT. For example, children who expressed embodied meanings of aggression toward others detected the first change sooner and detected more changes (outer orientation) when responding to the LSSOT versus the LSFT, indicating that their cognitive-emotional orientation focused on details in the environment related to aggression. In contrast children who did not experience-express embodied meanings of aggression toward others detected the first change sooner and more changes (outer orientation) with the LSFT versus the LSSOT, indicating their cognitive-emotional orientation focused on details in the environment related to affiliation. Another result raises an interesting question for future research. Children who experienced-expressed positive embodied meanings-emotions also perceived more changes on the person in the LSSOT scene who is being shot. Could children with positive embodied meanings experience more empathy, reflected by their unconsciously directing more attention at, and remembering more details about, the victim depicted in the LSSOT?

Discussion

In general the results of this study illustrate that with a normal population, a person's cognitive-emotional orientation is concordant with embodied meanings that are experienced and expressed.

DIALECTICAL RELATION BETWEEN COGNITIVE-EMOTIONAL ORIENTATION AND INSTRUMENTAL-EXPRESSIVE BEHAVIORS

The results of the studies of this probe are summarized in table 2.1. The first study explored the relation between cognitive-emotional orientation and the instrumental-expressive action mode. The second study explored the relation between cognitive-emotional orientation and the instrumental-expressive fantasy mode.

Study VI

Exploring the relation between cognitive-emotional orientation and the instrumental-expressive action mode. Participants were seventy-five children (thirty-five females; forty males; ages six to eighteen years) who had been admitted to an inpatient psychiatric facility.

Method

The participants were administered the LSSOT and the LSFT described in Study V. In addition the Binocular Test was devised to assess an instrumental-expressive behavior related to interpersonal interaction. With this procedure the examiner asked each participant to look at an object in the room through a pair of binoculars and experience how looking through one end of the binoculars magnifies the object and "moves it close to you," and looking at the object through the other end of the binoculars diminishes the object and "moves it away from you." Once the participant understood how to use the binoculars, the examiner stood about fifteen feet away and asked the participant to look at the examiner through whichever end of the binoculars the participant preferred to use.

Results

No age or gender differences were observed. Significant correlations were obtained only with the LSFT and the Binocular Test. Participants who looked through the binoculars to draw and experience the examiner closer detected fewer changes and later (inner Cognitive-Emotional Orientation). Participants who looked through the binoculars to move and experience the examiner further away detected more changes and sooner (outer Cognitive-Emotional Orientation). These results indicate that with this psychiatric population moving and experiencing the body of a person closer correlated with an inner cognitive orientation that focused on personal meanings-emotions related to interpersonal affiliation, while subordinating stimuli in the environment. In contrast, moving and experiencing the body of a person further away correlated with an outer cognitive orientation that focused on stimuli in the environment while subordinating personal meanings-emotions. From one point of view, this result suggests a lack of concordance displayed by this psychiatric population between the instrumental-expressive behavior of moving and experiencing a person nearer or farther away and the cognitive-emotional orientation that regulates interpersonal stimuli with those in the environment. Would a nonclinical population that moves-experiences a person further away display an inner orientation, indicating that they are focused on interpersonal needs while avoiding the external environment? Further studies will explore the relationships displayed by a nonclinical population with the Binocular Test, the LSSOT, and the LSFT.

This study, however, does make other contributions. It is important to note that no correlations were observed between performance with the Binocular Test and with the LSSOT, representing interpersonal aggression. The study also stimulates interest in the need to explore the relations between other instrumental-expressive behaviors and cognitive-emotional orientation. For example, a participant could be administered the LSSOT and the LSFT and then asked either to tie the examiners wrists with a rope, or help the examiner slip on a pair of gloves, to explore the relation between cognitive-emotional orientation and instrumental-expressive behaviors representing interpersonal aggression and affiliation.

Table 2.1. Fourth Probe: Relations between Instrumental-Expressive Behaviors and Cognitive-Emotional Orientations

STUDY	Instrumental-Expressive Behavior Experienced	Cognitive-Emotional Orientation Responding to a Scene of Interpersonal Interaction Representing	
		Affiliation	**Aggression**
VI	Move a Person Nearer to You	Inner	No Relation
	Move a Person Away from You	Outer	No Relation
VII	**Draw a Picture of Two Persons doing Something**		
	Picture of Aggression	Inner	Outer
	Picture of Friendship	Outer	Inner
VIII	**Discuss Events that Upset You**		
	Many Events	No Relation	Inner
	Few Events	No Relation	Outer
	Aggressive Events	No Relation	Inner

Study VII

This study was designed to explore the relation between Cognitive-Emotional Orientation and the Instrumental-Expressive Behavior of fantasizing persons interacting in some way.

Method

The Two-Person Drawing Test. With this procedure the examiner asks the participant to draw a picture of "two persons doing something." When the participant completes the drawing, the examiner notes, for example, "That's really good. Would you please tell me what's going on in your picture, so I can understand what you just drew." The drawings are rated in terms of three types of interpersonal interactions depicted: (1) aggression-competition from more to less direct (e.g. "This kid is kicking this kid." "These kids are racing to see who beats the other.") (2) Parallel activity either segregated or shared (e.g. "This kid is playing a game on his computer and this kid is reading." "These two girls are watching TV.") (3) Affiliation from less to more direct (e.g., "This kid is jumping rope, and this kid is clapping." "These kids are shaking hands.")

Participants were 185 public school children (grades K through 8). During a school day, with parental permission, each participant was administered The Two-Person Drawing Test and the LSSOT and LSFT. To balance the influence that the content of a leveling-sharpening test could have on the content of a participant's drawing, a particular sequence was followed. Half of the participants were administered the LSSOT first, than the Two-Person Drawing Test, and then the LSFT. The other half of the participants were administered the procedures in the reverse order.

Results

On the basis of his/her drawing, each participant was assigned to one of three groups: Aggressive Drawing Group, Parallel Drawing Group, and Affiliation Drawing Group. Participants whose drawings depicted two persons in an aggressive or vigorous competitive interaction detected more changes and sooner (outer cognitive-emotional orientation) with the LSSOT. In contrast, they detected fewer changes and later (inner cognitive-emotional orientation) with the LSFT. The participants whose drawings depicted two persons interacting in a friendly way produced opposite results. They detected more changes and sooner with the LSFT (outer cognitive-emotional orientation) and fewer changes and later with the LSSOT (inner cognitive-emotional orientation). The children whose drawings depicted two persons involved in parallel activity displayed the same cognitive-emotional orientation with the LSSOT and the LSFT.

The results of this study provide one illustration with a nonclinical population of how the process of a cognitive-emotional orientation interacts with, and is concordant with, the process of the fantasy mode of instrumental-expressive behaviors. When dealing with a scene depicting interpersonal violence (LSSOT), participants who had fantasized in their drawings interpersonal interactions as aggressive displayed an outer cognitive-emotional orientation that focused on and perceived many details that changed in the scene. When these participants were managing a scene depicting friendly, interpersonal interacting (LSFT), they shifted to an inner cognitive-emotional orientation that avoided the information in the environment and focused on inner meanings-fantasies. Conversely, the participants who had fantasized in their drawings friendly, interpersonal interactions, displayed an inner cognitive-emotional orientation when dealing with a scene depicting interpersonal aggression (LSSOT). This orientation enabled them to avoid the information presented by the environment while focusing on inner meanings. They also displayed an outer cognitive-emotional orientation when dealing with a scene depicting interpersonal affiliation, indicating they now focused on information presented by the environment. The Parallel Drawing Group displayed the same cognitive-emotional orientation with the LSSOT and LSFT. This illustrates that because these participants fantasize relationships as "side-by-side," rather than interacting, their cognitive-emotional orientation remains relatively impervious to changes in interpersonal interactions.

Study VIII

This study was designed to explore relations between cognitive-emotional orientations and the instrumental-expressive behavior of verbalizing-describing something that is upsetting.

Method

The Life Stressor Interview (LSI) described in Probe three and the LSSOT and LSFT.

The participants were 101 children attending an inner-city public school (grades K through 8; forty-three females; fifty-eight males). With parental permission and during a school day, each participant was individually administered the Life Stressor Interview, the LSSOT and the LSFT.

Results

All participants discussed at least one upsetting event, defining the following categories: (A) shootings or physical fights (N = 51); (B) verbal arguments (N = 50); (C) illness of a loved one (N = 48); (D) hospitalization of a loved one (N = 16); (E) death of a loved one (N = 33); (F) frustration of a wish (e.g., not being allowed to meet with friends) (N = 27). No differences in the types of upsetting events discussed were associated with age, gender, or grade level.

Performance with the LSFT did not relate to the number or type of upsetting events discussed. In contrast, participants who discussed more upsetting events (4–8) compared with those who discussed fewer upsetting events (1–3) displayed an inner Cognitive-Emotional Orientation with the LSSOT, focusing on inner meanings-emotions stimulated by the scene depicting violence. In addition, in terms of types of upsetting events discussed, only one resulted in a statistically significant difference. Children who discussed shootings and physical fights they had witnessed, or that took place nearby, displayed an inner cognitive-emotional orientation to a significant degree with the LSSOT. The results of this study suggest that the children who discussed many upsetting events, and who also discussed shootings and fights, probably experienced themselves surrounded by an environment that presented dangers. Accordingly, they coped by assuming an inner cognitive-emotional orientation that subordinated-avoided external environments. This issue relates to the studies summarized in the Fifth Probe of participants who were assessed while coping with environments that presented various challenges.

Discussion

The studies of this probe explored the second floor of the self-discussed in chapter 2 and illustrate that inner and outer cognitive-emotional orientations and instrumental-expressive behaviors of action, fantasy and language are correlated. The following are examples. In Study VI when asked to move the examiner nearer or farther away with a microaction (binoculars), this inpatient population displayed a relationship between this instrumental-expressive behavior and a cognitive-emotional orientation only when cognitively engaging a scene depicting friendship (LSFT) and not when cognitively engaging a scene depicting violence (LSSOT). Study VII illustrates that the instrumental-expressive fantasy mode and cognitive-emotional orientation are also correlated. For example, participants who expressed interpersonal-aggressive fantasies in their drawings of two persons doing something assumed an outer cognitive-emotional orientation when dealing with a scene (environment) depicting violence, indicating they focused on aggressive aspects of the outer world. In contrast when dealing with a scene (environment) depicting friendship (LSFT), they assumed an inner cognitive-emotional orientation that ignored-avoided this environment. Study VIII explored the relationship between cognitive-emotional orientation and the instrumental-expressive behavior of verbalizing. For example, participants who discussed many upsetting events displayed an inner cognitive-emotional orientation that subordinated-avoided information presented by a scene depicting violence (LSSOT) suggesting, as noted earlier, that they experienced themselves as surrounded by dangerous environments. This issue relates to the next probe that describes studies of participants coping with environments that present challenges and danger.

DIALECTICAL RELATIONS BETWEEN COGNITIVE-EMOTIONAL ORIENTATION AND USUAL AND UNUSUAL ENVIRONMENTS WITH WHICH A PERSON IS COPING-NEGOTIATING

In this probe several studies were conducted to explore the direction in which a person's cognitive-emotional orientation shifts when dealing with the calls for action from a familiar versus less familiar environment. In addition, and related to the discussion of the psychodynamic-relational view of environments presented in chapter 2, these studies were designed to explore changes (flexibility) in a person's cognitive-emotional orientation related to whether the call for action and stimulation presented by an environment is usual or unusual given the person's history, whether the environment restricts or permits active participation, and whether the person either elected or did not elect to enter the environment. These studies are summarized in table 2.2.

Table 2.2. Fifth Probe: Changes in Cognitive-Emotional Orientation Related to Negotiating Environments

STUDY	IX	X	XI	XII
Call for Action from Environment	Adults: Airport Prepare for Parachute Jump	Adults: Dorms Prepare for College Exam	Adults: Hospital Anticipate Surgery	Children: Hospital Anticipate Surgery
Participation Restricted	No	No	Yes	Yes
Call from Personal Meanings-Emotions	Be Safe – Focus on Environment Ignore Meanings-Emotions	Perform well – Focus on Environment Ignore Meanings-Emotions	To Cope – Focus on Meanings-Emotions Ignore Environment	To Cope – Focus on Meanings-Emotions Ignore Environment
Instrumental - Expressive Behavior Responding	Action	Action	Fantasy	Fantasy
Change in Cognitive-Emotional Orientation	Shift to Outer Orientation	Shift to Outer Orientation	Shift to Inner Orientation	Shift to Inner Orientation

Study IX. Preparing to Perform a Parachute Jump

This study explored the process of cognitive-emotional orientation while participants prepared to cope with the challenge, and calls for action, from an environment (parachute jumping) they had elected to enter. Forty-four male members of a parachute club, in their first phase of training, volunteered to participate. In the first phase of training, a member of the club is required to perform eight jumps with the following procedure. A static line is attached to the doorway of the airplane so that when the person jumps out from the airplane, the parachute is automatically opened. After this phase, the member takes a "free-fall jump." He jumps from the airplane and pulls a cord that releases the parachute.

All members of the club had performed two "static-line" jumps and agreed to participate in this study. Two groups were formed to serve the purpose of this study. The Experimental Group (N = 22) was scheduled to perform the third "static line jump" within a week. The Control Group (N = 22) had not yet been scheduled to perform the third static line jump.

Method

Two tests of the Leveling-Sharpening Cognitive-Emotional Regulator were constructed, replicating the makeup of the LSSOT and LSFT described in the Third Probe (i.e., sixty-three presentations of a scene, each displayed for five seconds, and twenty details gradually omitted). However, the tests constructed for this study presented stimuli related to parachute jumping. The Leveling-Sharpening Parachute Test: Form A presented a scene of a parachutist, whose parachute is not yet fully deployed, falling through space and performing a free-fall jump. The Leveling-Sharpening Parachute Test Form B presented a scene of a parachutist descending through space whose parachute is fully deployed. The Leveling-Sharpening House Test (LSHT) was also used because it did not contain any ingredients related to parachute jumping. The LSHT replicated the same format: sixty-three scenes of a house, each displayed for five seconds, and twenty details gradually omitted. Half of each group was administered the House Test after Parachute Test Form A and the other half after Parachute Test Form B.

Both Leveling Sharpening Parachute Tests and the LSHT were administered individually to each member of the Experimental Group on two occasions and in different locations to explore the influence of the surrounding environment, and its calls for action, on a person's cognitive-emotional orientation. The first location was the participant's home environment. The second administration took place seven days later at the airport within an hour of the participant boarding an airplane to perform the third static-line jump. The three tests were also administered individually to each member of the Control Group at first in his home environment and seven days later again in his home environment.

Results

The results obtained make a vivid contribution to the issue of the importance of flexibility a person's cognitive-emotional orientation displays, as the person copes with the calls for action from different environments. When at the airport, compared to their performance in their home environments, the members of the Experimental Group shifted significantly to an outer orientation with both Parachute Tests and the House Test (i.e., they detected the first change sooner, detected more changes, and lagged less in detecting a change once it is introduced). The Control Group showed no differences between the first and second evaluation with each test. This result suggests that when a person engages a familiar environment (home), and then engages another environment the person elected to enter that presents calls for actions the person must manage to negotiate safety, and does not impose restrictions, the leveling-sharpening cognitive-emotional regulator shifts flexibly to an outer orientation. This orientation focuses on the environment being managed while subordinating personal meanings-emotions.

Another finding is especially related to this issue. When performance in each environment with the two Parachute Tests were compared, significant differences were obtained with the Experimental Group but not with the Control Group. In contrast to their performance when in a home environment, at the airport the members of the Experimental Group displayed a significantly greater outer orientation (i.e., detected more changes and sooner) with Parachute Test Form A. (a scene of a parachutist performing a free-fall jump) than with Form B. (parachutist slowly drifting down with parachute fully deployed). This result suggests that since none of the participants had yet experienced a free-fall jump, the free-fall scene stimulated the following: to ensure personal safety be as alert as possible to all information presented by the environment and avoid, subordinate personal meanings-emotions.

Another result is related to this issue. Recall that half of the Experimental Group was administered the House Test after they had experienced dealing with Parachute Test Form A (free fall) and the other half after they had experienced Parachute Test Form B (slow decent). Participants of the Experimental Group who responded to the House Test immediately after they had responded to the free fall scene, showed a significantly greater shift to an outer orientation with the House Test than did participants of the Experimental Group who responded to the House Test after the slow decent scene. This finding suggests that for a novice parachutist, a picture itself of someone performing a free-fall jump stimulates his cognitive emotional orientation to maintain an outer orientation and be alert to all information in the environment, while subordinating personal meanings-emotions.

Study X: Anticipating and Preparing for a College Course Exam

Related to Study IX, this study also explored the process of cognitive-emotional orientation when persons anticipate and prepare to cope with the calls for action presented by an environment they had elected to engage, and that is usual and does not impose restrictions. College students (twenty-two females; twenty-two males; age nineteen to twenty-four) attending a summer session at a university volunteered to participate. Two groups were organized in terms of whether or not they were anticipating taking a final exam in two weeks. Twenty-two of the participants (eleven males and eleven females) who were scheduled to take a final examination formed the Experimental Group. Twenty-two participants (eleven males and eleven females) who were not scheduled to take a final exam in two weeks formed the Control Group.

Method

The Leveling Sharpening House Test (LSHT) was used to evaluate the Cognitive-Emotional Orientation of the participants. Stimulated by the results obtained with this procedure when participants coped with preparing for a parachute jump (Study IX), the House Test was used to explore whether or not a person's Cognitive Emotional Orientation could be assessed with stimuli that were not related to the stimuli in the environment being negotiated. The LSHT was administered individually to each participant in his/her dormitory room and again two weeks later in his/her dormitory room. At the second evaluation the participants of the Experimental Group were scheduled to take a final exam within twenty-four hours. At the start of this evaluation, the examiner engaged the participant in a discussion for a few minutes to stimulate meanings-emotions related to anticipating the final exam. For example, "How tough do you think your exam is going to be?" "Do you think you're ready for this final exam?" At the start of the second evaluation with the participants of the Control Group, the examiner made general comments, for example, "How are things going?"

Results

In the first evaluation, the participants of the two groups did not differ in their performance with the LSHT. In addition, the Control Group did not show any difference in their second performance with the LSHT compared to their first performance. In contrast, during the second evaluation, compared to the first, the Experimental Group showed a significant shift to an outer orientation; namely they detected more changes and detected a change sooner once it was introduced into the series of pictures. This result added support to the concept that when a person engages the calls for action from a usual environment she/he elected to enter that does not restrict active participation, and then engages the environment again whose calls for action emphasize the need to cope successively, a cognitive-emotional orientation flexibly shifts temporarily to an outer orientation to manage and serve those calls for action from the environment and inner self. The next two studies introduce another important dimension to this process.

Study XI: Adults Anticipating and Preparing to Undergo Surgery

This study addresses the issue of changes in cognitive-emotional orientation when a person is negotiating an environment she/he did not elect to enter, that is unusual and restricts active participation. All participants of this study volunteered, forming two groups. Group A consisted of fifteen hospitalized males (mean age thirty-two years) who were scheduled for surgery that was to take place within twenty-four hours of the evaluation of their Cognitive-Emotional Orientation. Group B consisted of twenty males (mean age forty-seven years) who were patients at the same hospital, but were not scheduled for a surgical procedure.

Method

To evaluate the leveling sharpening cognitive-emotional regulator with stimuli related to a hospital environment, the Leveling-Sharping Hospital Test was constructed. The scene consisted of a doctor in a hospital room who is holding a syringe upward in one hand, and standing near the foot of a bed and a table on which are located several medical items. Following the format of the other procedures, the LS Hospital Test consisted of sixty-three scenes with twenty details deleted beginning with scene 3, each scene presented for five seconds. The LS House Test was also administered to evaluate a participant's Cognitive-Emotional Orientation when stimuli have no relation to the environment being negotiated. The LS Hospital Test and The LS House Test were administered individually to the participants of both groups in their hospital room.

Results

With the LS Hospital Test, the participants of Group A (anticipating surgery) displayed an inner orientation to a significantly higher degree (i.e., detected fewer changes and later). The performance of Group B (hospitalized but not anticipating surgery) also displayed an inner orientation but to a lesser degree. Results obtained with the LS House Test paralleled those obtained with the Hospital Test, but did not reach the same level of statistical significance. This result illustrates that when a person negotiates the calls for action from an environment that is not usual and restricts participation, Cognitive-Emotional Orientation shifts to an inner orientation, ignoring the calls for action from the environment and focusing on the calls from the inner self.

Study XII: Children Anticipating and Managing Surgery or Dental Repair

This study provided another opportunity to explore changes that occur in a person's cognitive-emotional orientation when negotiating the calls for action from an unusual environment the person did not elect to enter and that restricts activity. The exploration of this issue is elaborated by including two additional features: (1) The parents of the participants who were hospitalized and experienced surgery provided observations and opinions about the behavior of their children before and after surgery; (2) In addition to assessing the Cognitive-Emotional Orientation of participants, procedures were used to evaluate the meanings-emotions expressed by the instrumental-expressive fantasy mode.

The participants formed three groups. The Surgical Group consisted of fifteen boys (mean age nine years) who were attending a public school and scheduled to be hospitalized for hernia repair. The Dental Group consisted of fifteen boys (mean age nine years) who were attending public school and scheduled to see a dentist for the first time to repair tooth decay. The Control Group consisted of fifteen boys (mean age nine years) who were attending public school and who had no major events scheduled. All children participated with parental permission, and their histories did not indicate any psychological difficulties.

Method

The children of each group were evaluated individually with the same procedures on three occasions. The children of the Surgical Group were evaluated in their homes one week before hospitalization (Time 1), and again when in a hospital room one day before the scheduled surgery (Time 2), and again in their homes three weeks after being discharged from the hospital (Time 3). The children of the Dental Group were evaluated in their homes one week before their dental appointments (Time 1), and again at the dentist's office (Time 2), and again at home three weeks after dental repair (Time 3). The children of the Control Group were evaluated in their homes (Time 1), again one week later (Time 2), and again three weeks later (Time 3). An important feature of this study involved semi-structured interviews held with each mother of a child in the Surgical Group that took place at her home during Time 1 and Time 3. Each mother was encouraged to share her observations and opinions as to whether or not, and to what degree, her child displayed behavior related to various categories; for example anxiety, moodiness, difficulty sleeping, or reluctance to stepping outside and exploring the neighborhood.

The Leveling-Sharpening Hospital Test (described in Study X) and the Leveling-Sharpening House Test were used to evaluate the cognitive-emotional orientation each child displayed at Times 1, 2, and 3. In addition, two other procedures were administered to assess a child's concern-anxiety about his personal safety expressed by the instrumental-expressive fantasy mode: (A) The Fables Test. With this procedure the examiner read a brief story about a monkey who is very proud of his big, pretty tail. When the monkey's keeper arrives, he notices that the tail looks different. At this point, the examiner asks, "What do you think could have happened?" Responses were ranked from fantasies representing direct injury (e.g., "The tail was chopped off.") to fantasies representing attenuated, delayed expressions (e.g., "Like the hair was clipped off."). (B) The Picture Test. With this procedure the examiner placed before the child Card 18GF of the Thematic Apperception Test (TAT) that depicts two persons, one with their hands near the neck of the other. The examiner asked the child to look at the picture and make up a story about what is going on. Responses were rated from fantasies depicting one person engaged in aggressive behavior toward the other (e.g., "Looks like this person is about to strangle that one.") to fantasies depicting interpersonal affiliation-compassion (e.g., "I think this person's lips hurt, and this person is going to look them over to help."

Results

The results obtained with these procedures parallel those of Study XI and also offer important elaborations. At Time 1 the performance of the Surgical Group, the Dental Group, and the Control Group with the Leveling-Sharpening Hospital Test and the Leveling-Sharpening House Test did not differ, reflecting the same cognitive-emotional orientation. In addition, the Control Group displayed the same cognitive-emotional orientation during the second evaluation (one week later) and the third evaluation (three weeks later). In sharp contrast, at Time 2, the Surgical Group shifted the most to an inner cognitive-emotional orientation with both tests, but to a higher degree with the Leveling-Sharpening Hospital Test than the Leveling-Sharpening House Test. (i.e., they perceived fewer changes in the scene and perceived changes much later after they were introduced). The Dental Group showed the same trend at Time 2 but to a lesser degree. At Time 3, three weeks after leaving the hospital, the Surgical Group displayed the same inner Cognitive-Emotional Orientation they had displayed when in the hospital. The Dental Group showed the same trend but to a lesser degree.

Other important results were obtained with the Fables Test and TAT card that assessed whether or not changes took place with the instrumental-expressive fantasy mode, and whether these changes related to changes in cognitive-emotional orientation. When at the hospital (Time 2) versus when at home (Time 1), the responses of the Surgical Group to the Fables Test showed a significant increase in fantasies that expressed direct forms of aggression and body harm (e.g., "The tail was chopped off."). A significant increase in fantasies representing interpersonal aggression was also revealed by their responses to TAT card 18GF (e.g., "Now when I look at this picture, it looks like she's about to slap her face.") The Dental Group produced the same results but to a lower level of statistical significance. The fantasies expressed by the Control Group at Time 1 and Time 2 showed no change. These results indicate that because the Leveling-Sharpening Cognitive-Emotional Regulator flexibly shifted to an inner orientation when the Surgical Group was in the hospital, this shift facilitated their expressing and rehearsing with fantasies meanings-emotions representing concerns about body harm. The next result obtained adds significance to this process

Recall that each mother of the children in the Surgical Group was interviewed at Time 1 and again at Time 3 to obtain her observations of her child's behavior. The data obtained make an important contribution to the concept regarding the relations among embodied meanings, cognitive-emotional orientation, instrumental-expressive behaviors and environments. Significant correlations were obtained. At Time 1 the higher the degree of an outer cognitive-emotional orientation a child showed with the Leveling-Sharpening Tests the more the mother rated the child as less anxious, less irritable, more cooperative and more free to venture outside. The correlations obtained at Time 3 (three weeks after hospitalization) were in the *opposite* direction. Children whose performance at Time 3 with the Leveling-Sharpening Tests showed the most inner cognitive-emotional orientation correlated significantly with their mothers rating them, for example, as less anxious and irritable and more cooperative.

The relevance of this result is clarified if the results obtained with the fantasy tests, when these children were in the hospital, are considered. Recall that these children, who were about to undergo surgery, showed that their inner cognitive-emotional orientation correlated with expressing fantasies representing body injury and aggressive interpersonal interactions. Combining the results of Time 2 and Time 3 leads to the following inference. Because the hospital environment was stressful, unusual and restrictive, flexibly shifting to an inner cognitive-emotional orientation provided the opportunity for embodied meanings-emotions representing fear of body harm to be expressed, rehearsed and negotiated in fantasies. Accordingly, shifting flexibly to an inner cognitive-emotional orientation when in the hospital, maintaining this orientation three weeks later while recovering from surgery, and at the same time continuing to engage in fantasies that expressed-negotiated fear of bodily harm, contributed to each child being less anxious and irritable, and more free to venture outside.

The results of this study lead to the following concept. When a person is coping with a stressful, unusual environment that limits taking some action, the flexible reorganizing of a cognitive-emotional regulator to an inner orientation is associated with elements of the inner-self (e.g., fantasizing) that contribute to coping successfully with the stressful environment. We noted earlier that the instrumental-expressive fantasy mode provides a person with alternative opportunities to negotiate goals when the environment does not provide opportunities for the person to take some action. The results of this study support the view that when a person is coping with an environment that limits action, if the person expresses and rehearses meanings-emotions in the fantasy mode, the person's inner self has the opportunity to continue negotiating the issue in question. We consider therapy cases in chapter 4 that illustrate if developmental interferences persist for a long time versus a few days during early development, they result in the person developing a very rigid inner or outer cognitive-emotional orientation that governs the person's interactions with all environments and prevents the opportunity for instrumental-expressive action, fantasy and language modes to rehearse and revise meanings.

Discussion

The results obtained illustrate that flexibility in cognitive-emotional orientation, and a dialectical relationship between this flexible orientation and instrumental-expressive behaviors increase successful coping. This is especially true when a person is dealing with the calls for action from her/his usual environment and then required to cope with the calls for action from unusual environments. The results also illustrate that cognitive-emotional flexibility relates to engaging instrumental-expressive behavioral modes, such as fantasizing, that contribute to coping successfully.

The issue of the positive influence of dialectical relations among embodied meanings, cognitive-emotional orientations, instrumental-expressive behaviors and environments is further illustrated by a study colleagues and I conducted (Santostefano et. al., 2006). In this study 106 children (ages nine to nineteen years), residing in a village maintained by the Spanish government for abandoned children, were evaluated. Of this population, forty-eight of the children had been invited a number of times by relatives to visit them (Home Group). The remaining children (fifty-eight) had not experienced visits to the homes of relatives (Village Group). All children were administered the Life Stressor Interview described in Study VIII. Significant differences were obtained between the responses of the Home Group and the Village Group, supporting the relational view noted in chapter 2. For example, the participants who were provided the opportunity to spend time with and visit relatives (Home Group) discussed less often being upset by aggressive events and discussed more often being upset by the death of a loved one.

CONCLUDING COMMENT

In general, the results of the studies summarized in this chapter support the point of view that the matrix of psychological processes discussed in chapter 1 play a key role in psychological functioning and hold special significance for psychotherapy, especially if these processes have been disrupted by developmental interferences. I hope the research studies reviewed in this chapter provide a therapist with another lens through which to examine whether cognitive and behavioral aspects of a person, who is being considered for psychoanalytic-relational psychotherapy, are disconnected or interrelated. The glasses also focus on whether a person experiences and responds to various persons and environments in the same way or with reflexivity. In contrast to the participants of the studies presented, especially studies IX to XII, the therapy cases described in chapter 4 illustrate that if a person during childhood experiences other persons and environments imposing severe restrictions, the links connecting embodied meanings, cognitive-emotional regulators and instrumental-expressive behaviors are broken, and a very rigid inner or outer cognitive-emotional orientation develops, in addition to a very rigid instrumental-expressive action or fantasy or language behavior. In addition, this rigidity governs the person's interactions with all environments and prevents adequate functioning. The therapy cases are presented to illustrate why particular enactments are necessary to reestablish those links.

THREE

Clinical Illustrations of Relational-Psychotherapy

Revising Rigid Cognitive-Emotional Orientations and Instrumental-Expressive Behaviors with Enactments

In this chapter I summarize the psychotherapy I conducted with an adult, an adolescent, and a child to illustrate therapeutic techniques that serve persons who are handicapped by a very rigid cognitive-emotional orientation and rigid instrumental-expressive behavior, resulting from traumatic experiences. This rigidity dictated why these individuals interacted with all environments with the same meanings-emotions and behavior and interfered significantly with their being able to interact with others and environments in a positive way. Related to the focus of this volume, what these patients repeated cognitively-emotionally and behaviorally during interactions with me and other persons derived from a very rigid inner or outer cognitive-emotional orientation and rigid instrumental-expressive behavior that masked-disguised the traumatic embodied meanings the person was avoiding. Each case illustrates why and when a therapist should prescribe, initiate, and participate in enactments with a patient to launch an embodied, interpersonal process that enables the patient to experience and eventually resolve the embodied meanings that are the source of the cognitive-emotional and behavioral rigidity. The cases also illustrate that as enactments are repeated the traumatic embodied meanings are gradually re-experienced and resolved, contributing to the development of a more flexible cognitive-emotional orientation and instrumental-expressive behavior that facilitate the patient's understanding, insight, and positive interaction with persons and environments.

Before each case is reviewed, it should be useful if we consider a brief overview of the psychoanalytic concept of therapeutic action. In a discussion of what he considered acting out, Freud (1914) noted that what cannot be remembered will be repeated in action in the patient's here and now behavior with the analyst. Related to this issue, decades ago Hans Loewald (1960) emphasized, in a publication frequently cited, that the process of change in analytic therapy is "set in motion not simply by the technical skill of the analyst, but by the fact that the analyst makes himself available for the development of a new object relationship . . . " (p. 224). Illustrated by the cases presented in this chapter, I emphasize that with persons who present a very rigid cognitive-emotional orientation and very rigid instrumental-expressive behavior the therapist often cannot make himself adequately available with verbal discourse. In order to develop a new relationship, these individuals may require the opportunity to engage in new body experiences. From this viewpoint to make himself/herself available, a therapist may use his/her body and invite the patient to join the activity and use his/her body.

My proposal relates to the following viewpoint expressed by Beebe and Lachman (2014) based upon their comprehensive and innovative research that investigated mothers and infants interacting: "Although psychoanalysis tends to focus on the linguistic content of communication, it is now increasingly understood that bodily or implicit aspects of communication is not only necessary for communication with language . . . but is an essential component of the very capacity to communicate and understand emotion . . . " (p. xvii). My proposal also relates to Pine (1998) pointing out that the techniques used to promote change in analytic therapy should be designed according to the characteristics of the patient and the analyst. In addition my proposal is especially related to Aron's (1998a) discussion of "The Clinical Body and the Reflexive Mind" (p. 3). He notes, for example, that although the psychoanalytic process is often thought to be focused on self-awareness and psychological mindedness, of equal importance, "The body, bodily sensations, bodily experiences, bodily metaphors and bodily imagery play a central role in the psychoanalytic process" (p. 3). From this point of view, he elaborates on the importance of "Self-reflexivity (i.e., the capacity to experience, observe, and reflect on oneself as both a subject and an object) . . . " (p. 3), and addresses the issue that trauma disrupts self-reflexivity and interpersonal interactions. I proposed, and illustrated with the studies described in chapter 2, how the processes of cognitive-emotional orientation and instrumental-expressive behavior that develop from body experiences, play a key role in self-reflexivity.

Another issue related to the clinical cases reviewed in this chapter is addressed by Gabbard and Western (2003). In their discussion of therapeutic action they emphasize that a theory of therapeutic action must describe what changes (i.e., the aims of treatment) and what strategies are likely to be useful in facilitating these changes (i.e., the techniques of the treatment). In response to this recommendation, the therapy cases presented in this chapter illustrate that to modify the rigid cognitive-emotional orientation and rigid instrumental-instrumental expressive behavior a patient displays and to cultivate reflexivity (the aim of treatment), the therapist should prescribe, initiate, and participate in enactments with the patient (the technique). As these enactments are repeated, they provide the patient with body experiences that gradually promote flexibility in the patient's cognitive-emotional orientation and instrumental-expressive behavior. As a result the patient's reflexivity improves which equips the patient to eventually address, revise, and resolve embodied meanings related to past traumatic experiences that had been the foundation of the patient's self and the source of psychological problems. At this point we take a closer look at the therapeutic technique of enactment.

ENACTING EMBODIED METAPHORS: THE LANGUAGE THAT REVISES RIGID COGNITIVE-EMOTIONAL ORIENTATIONS, INSTRUMENTAL-EXPRESSIVE BEHAVIORS AND DEVELOPS REFLEXIVITY

At the core of the technique of enacting is the issue, noted earlier, that the cognitive-emotional orientation and instrumental-expressive behavior of a person who experienced traumatic events lack flexibility when responding to the calls for action from embodied meanings and environments. Aron's (1998b) discussion of how trauma interferes with self-reflexive functioning is related. He reviews adults who are unable to experience and express feelings, and share the way they interpret some event, because the trauma they experienced has broken the link between the Me-Self that experiences and the I-Self that observes and interprets experiences. Accordingly, Aron notes that these persons are left "anesthetized, out of touch with their feelings and emotions" (p. 15) and are "unable to utilize their body sensations . . . traumatized patients are unable to reflect on their traumatic experiences, and self-reflexive functioning fails" (p. 25). In terms of the model presented in chapter 2, this failure relates to flaws that occurred in the development of a Core-Self and an identity. Relying on his research with infants and the research by Sander and Piaget (noted in chapter 2), Stern (2002) notes, "I argue that identification remains as central to psychological life as Freud thought" (p. 723). He also emphasizes that developing a sense of self by identifying with others is so critical for psychological development that it is "something analogous to our need for oxygen . . . I view identification as fundamental to life" (p. 725).

If we integrate Aron's (1998b) view that traumatic experiences disrupt the dialectical relationship between a person's I-Self and Me-Self with infant research that emphasizes the importance of a child negotiating and identifying with caregivers, the embodied meanings representing a person's traumatic experiences eclipse positive relationships the person has available. In addition, given that the link between the I-Self and Me-Self has been broken, the I-Self fails to make use of meanings of available non traumatic experiences that could revise the original traumatic meaning. As a result the person repeatedly gives the same meanings to experiences, repeats behaviors that do not reciprocate-negotiate with others, and expects particular responses from relationships. At this point the question arises, "What is the best way to help a person whose link between the I-Self and Me-Self is broken?" This question relates to the surge of interest that has been stimulated by relational psychoanalysis. Instead of a therapist focusing on verbally discussing and interpreting the meanings of this patient's behavior, interacting and enacting with this patient are the main vehicles of change (e.g., Frank, 1999). As Aron (1996) stated, "In interpersonal psychoanalytic work the focus is on what a patient does with the analyst, how the patient is being with the analyst, rather than predominantly on what the patient is saying to the analyst" (p. 75). I embrace this proposal, but also stress that it is equally important to focus on what the therapist does with the patient, and how the therapist enacts with the patient, to make himself/herself available as an object with which the patient can identify. In addition, interpersonal enactments provide the patient the opportunity to accumulate body experiences producing positive meanings that revise and replace embodied meanings representing traumatic experiences. From this proposal we pause to define the concept of enactment.

What is an Enactment?

Interest in using enactments during psychotherapy with adults and children has increased, and different definitions have been proposed to address body expressions that occur during interactions. (e.g., McLaughlin, 1991; Ellman and Moskowitz, 1998; Frank, 2002; Grossmark, 2012). As I use the term, an *enactment* consists of a constellation of physical actions involving the therapist's body and nearby objects that the therapist initiates and performs to express a particular meaning, and invites the patient to participate. There are two broad phases in this process that involve five technical steps detailed in chapter 4. During the first phase, the constellation of actions introduced by the therapist expresses a particular embodied meaning that symbolizes and replicates the rigid instrumental-expressive behavior and cognitive-emotional orientation the patient has been displaying. During the second phase, the therapist introduces constellations of actions that stimulate and express different embodied meanings designed to promote flexibility in the patient's rigid cognitive-emotional orientation and rigid instrumental-expressive behavior and that eventually result in the patient reliving and resolving the trauma. The viewpoint that change in psychological processes is promoted by patient and therapist participating together while enacting embodied meanings was proposed decades ago by Sandor Ferenczi, a controversial figure in the early years of classical psychoanalysis. Ferenczi's contribution is emphasized by Aron (1996) who noted, "Sixty years after his clinical experiments . . . we . . . find new veins of gold" (pp. 160–161) . . . "Not only did he anticipate our contemporary views (i.e., those of relational psychoanalysis), but we still have to catch up to his insights" (p. 169). Another statement by Aron (1998b) is especially related to my proposal that the therapist author and initiate an enactment. He noted, "Gradually patient and analyst mutually regulate each other's behavior . . . such that each gets under the other's skin . . . the analyst must be attuned to the nonverbal, the affective . . . [and] to his or her body responses, so that these may be . . . gradually utilized to construct metaphors and symbols that may be . . . exchanged by [patient and therapist]" (p. 26).

Related to this important issue, I illustrate with the therapy cases presented in this chapter that patients who are handicapped by a very rigid cognitive-emotional orientation and very rigid instrumental-expressive behavior are unable to get under the therapist's skin, and their rigidity prevents the therapist from getting under the patient's skin. What can the therapist do to promote the process of patient and therapist getting under each other's skin? My response is that the therapist must initiate a series of enactments designed to promote interactions involving the bodies of the patient and therapist. These interactions initially provide experiences representing particular embodied meanings related to the patient's rigidity, and then provide embodied experiences representing flexibility. This interactive process enables the patient to gradually internalize the symbols-metaphors represented by the patient's and therapist's body activities and develop a new self. In addition, following the matrix of concepts presented in chapter 1, as the pathological foundation of the patient's embodied meanings is revised, flexibility in cognitive-emotional orientation and instrumental-expressive behavior increases when responding to the calls for action from environments. This proposal relates to Aron (1996) pointing out that "[Relational therapists] . . . believe that what is the most important is that the patient has a new experience rooted in a new relationship . . . " (p. 214). The relational concept that a patient should have a new experience rooted in a new relationship relates to a major part of my proposal, namely that enactments must be repeated until the patient's embodied meanings, cognition, emotion, and behavior indicate that his/her new self is having new experiences and new relationships.

The Importance of Repeating Enactments

I emphasize that one or two enactments in which patient and therapist participate do not make a sufficient contribution. The research by Piaget, Stern, and Sander reviewed in chapter 1, and especially the research by Beebe and Lachman (2014), emphasize that infants and toddlers repeat cycles of interactions with caregivers many times, resulting in the construction of embodied meanings-emotions. Also as noted in chapter 1, when infants and children are exposed to developmental interferences, meanings representing these traumatic experiences are constructed at the body level, not in images-fantasies and words. In addition, related to Aron's (1998a) discussion noted earlier, the links connecting these traumatic embodied meanings, cognitive-emotional processes, and instrumental-expressive behaviors are broken, so that these traumatic embodied meanings cannot be rehearsed, negotiated and revised with actions, fantasies and words (see Study XII in chapter 2). To construct links that connect these modes, enactments must be repeated many times, demonstrated by infant research. Illustrated by the therapy cases that follow, repeating a series of enactments many times establishes links among the modes of embodied meanings, cognitive-emotional orientation and instrumental-expressive behavior, and also between the patient's I-Self and Me-Self. Once these links are established early embodied, traumatic meanings are experienced and eventually revised and resolved.

THERAPY CASE 1

LARRY: A VERY RIGID INNER COGNITIVE-EMOTIONAL ORIENTATION AND RIGID INSTRUMENTAL-EXPRESSIVE BEHAVIOR

Larry, age thirty-eight, requested a consultation. During our first meeting, he pointed out that he had been in psychotherapy two sessions per week for a year. He decided to terminate more than six months ago because he did not find it helpful. He also noted that a colleague, who works for the same accounting firm and who had been in psychoanalysis with me, suggested that Larry consider meeting with me. I responded that it would help me be of help if he shared some of the reasons why he had arranged for psychotherapy a couple of years ago. He reached into his pocket and pulled out a sheet of paper, held it in both hands, and slowly read a list of "problems" he has with his wife, children, and at the accounting firm where he works. The following are examples of the problems he shared during this and the next two sessions, slowly reading items he had listed on sheets of paper.

Regarding his wife, Larry noted that they have been having problems from the time they were married. For example, she gets upset because every day before he leaves for work, he approaches her with a sheet of paper on which he has written a list of items he plans to handle during the day, and insists she listen to the list so she has a sense of what he plans to do. She also gets upset for the following reasons: he frequently complains that she places his clothing in the wrong locations of his closet; at dinnertime he checks the location of the silverware she has placed at the side of each plate to ensure that the space between them is correct; he does not spontaneously help her, for example, emptying the dishwasher or folding laundry. Larry reported several times that his wife frequently says, "Larry, I feel like we're not together and you're not here."

Regarding his children, Larry noted that he has an eight-year-old son and five-year-old daughter and commented, "I don't know why I also have problems with my kids. I like them, but I find it hard to play with them." He added that his son enjoys learning to play chess and often asks Larry to give him "another lesson." Whenever they do play a game, his son complains because Larry frequently corrects the location of chess pieces to ensure each is set exactly in the center of the square. Before dinner time, sometimes Larry asks his son and daughter to place napkins next to each plate, and then checks to see if "all is OK." His wife gets upset and frequently asks, "Larry, why are you always checking? What the kids do is fine."

Carefully following his list of items, Larry noted, "I have been having problems where I work for a long time." He slowly read and added comments to each of the following incidents that occurred at the accounting firm where he works. The director of the unit in which Larry works has insisted several times that when the members of the unit have a meeting, Larry must remain seated until the meeting is over. Larry added that for reasons he does not understand, minutes before a meeting is scheduled to come to a close, frequently he stands up, collects his papers and walks out of the conference room. "I get up and leave because for me it seems like what we're discussing is over." Another item related to his work setting concerned a colleague whom he supervises and who gets upset when Larry insists that he place particular documents in certain locations that Larry designated. Larry added, "This guy keeps saying I don't feel you're connected at all with me. You're all about where I put the papers."

After Larry described these details, I noted that it would also help me if he shared why he decided to terminate psychotherapy. Larry responded, "I always brought a list with me to make sure I covered the issues that I thought were important. All that therapist kept doing was explain why I made the list of things to talk about. Like he kept saying maybe there are other things you should remember, but you're pushing them away because you don't want to talk about them." I offered to help

Larry and proposed that he consider psychoanalysis so he can explore if it helps compared to his previous experience. He responded in a positive way, shared that he knows psychoanalysis meant lying down on a couch four sessions a week, and added his colleague had told him that it helped him a lot.

As I had anticipated, during each session of the first three weeks, Larry lay down on the couch, took a sheet of paper out of his pocket, carefully spread it open, and commented, "Well, this is what I want to talk about today." The number of items he had listed varied from session to session. Larry usually began by announcing the number of items on the list, and then carefully read each one in order, adding details. His very rigid cognitive-emotional orientation was displayed by the content of each item on the list that he described in molecular detail. His very rigid instrumental expressive behavior was displayed by his bringing a list to every session, announcing the number of items on the list, carefully adjusting the position of his body on the couch to ensure that it was located on the center, and carefully reading each item. During these sessions I used typical strategies to foster a therapeutic process, help Larry free associate and discover what his nonverbal behavior was expressing. For example, after he read an item on the list and added details, I commented, "Larry, sorry, I know I'm going to sound like the therapist you left last year. Before you read the next item, let's see if what you just read reminds you of anything else that happened." Larry paused for about thirty seconds, and continued reading the next item. As another example, at the start of a session, after lying on the couch, Larry held up the sheet of paper and exclaimed, "Here it is. I brought another list of things for us to think about." I chuckled, "Larry, sorry but again I'm going to sound like that therapist you left. Before you start reading what's on that list, please join me in a game." I explained that because his list could be blocking other thoughts from saying what they want to say, the game is to place the list to one side, close his eyes, let his mind relax for two minutes, and see if any other thoughts flash into his mind. I added I would let him know when two minutes are up. Larry laughed, "Even though you sound like that other therapist, at least you're making it a game. So let's do it." After I mentioned that two minutes had passed, he replied, "Sorry. Nothing else came up. The only things I thought about are what I wrote on the list that I brought today." I tried techniques like this for several sessions, but each time obtained the same result. None of these interventions seemed to help Larry be more flexible and free associate. On occasion, I felt disappointed and irritated because of my failure, a feeling that must have influenced my tone. At the start of one session when he walked in with his sheet of paper in hand, I commented, "Another list." Larry responded, "What's the matter? You sound pissed off." I apologized and tried to convey with a positive tone that I was interested in learning about the items he brought today. Also, to handle my frustration, because of my experiences with the benefit of activity and the outdoors, I asked Larry if he wanted to take a brief walk outside. With a firm tone, he replied, "No," got on the couch, and spread out his sheet of paper. I realized I made an error and that there was much to be done before Larry would join me for a walk.

I began working with Larry a few months after a book was released (i.e., *Relational Perspectives of the Body*, 1998, edited by Aron and Anderson) that I had read with much interest, given my personal experiences discussed in the Preface, as well as my professional experiences with the Miniature Situations Test and the Action Test of Body Image described in chapter 2. I had already become very committed to the viewpoint of relational psychoanalysis as presented, for example, by Lou Aron in his 1996 volume, *A Meeting of the Minds: Mutuality in Psychoanalysis* which I also had read with much interest. Given my commitment to the viewpoint of relational psychoanalysis, and that embodied meanings form the foundation of a person's self, because my efforts to help Larry free associate were not successful, I decided to introduce micro body enactments to cultivate a shared interactive language with Larry. If we achieved some success, I would then consider enactments providing embodied experiences that could cultivate flexibility in his rigid cognitive-emotional orientation and rigid instrumental-expressive behavior.

At the start of the next session, when Larry entered the office and walked toward the couch, I held up a sheet of paper. Larry asked, "What's that? You never had a sheet of paper before, when I walked in." I replied, "I know I sounded irritated when we met last time. To add to my apology I decided to try to be like you." I added that I made a list of things that came into my thoughts after our last meeting so I could mention them today. I showed Larry my list and he smiled. At the start of each of the following sessions, I showed him that I brought my list as he had. Larry's tone gradually became more positive so that on a couple of occasions, when he entered the office and before I showed him my list, he asked "Can I take a look at your list?" and noted the number of items I had written. Because of his positive tone, I decided to add a detail to the microbody enactment we were sharing. When Larry arrived I showed him that I had placed a check mark at the end of each item on my list. I explained that after I composed the list, I examined each item to see if it needed editing. If the item was OK, I wrote a check mark. I handed Larry a pencil, asked him to look over the items he had listed and make a check mark after each one, if it didn't need any changes. With some irritation in his tone Larry asked, "Why are you asking me to do that?" I replied that I was trying to figure out other ways that might make us feel like we are "walking together." Larry took the pencil, reviewed his list, and made check marks. When Larry arrived for the next session, he smiled and showed me that he had reviewed and made check marks by each item on his list. He repeated this for the next four sessions, and I also showed him the check marks on my list.

Given Larry's positive attitude, I decided to introduce a minor elaboration to our microbody enactment to explore whether it would contribute to our developing a shared interactive language. When Larry entered the office, I again showed him my list and noted that I decided to write a number at the start of each item, instead of a check mark at the end of the item. I explained that, after reviewing the list of items, I wrote the number one at the start of the most important item, the number two at the start of the next most important item and so on. I asked Larry if he wanted to do the same with his list. He responded with interest and devoted several minutes examining his list, ranking his items and writing numbers. At the start of the next session when Larry arrived, he showed me with pride that he had written numbers, ranking the items on his list, and I showed him that I had done the same. We repeated this at the start of the next three sessions. When Larry arrived for the following session, he showed me his list and with pride noted he had elaborated what we had been doing. He explained that after reviewing the items and writing a number next to each, he decided to rewrite the list so that the number one item is at the top of the page, item number two next and so on. Larry asked me to rewrite my list in the same way which I did with a very positive tone. I was very pleased that Larry initiated an addition to our enactment, and asked me to participate, because it confirmed that we were developing a shared interactive language and a reciprocal relationship. At the start of the next four sessions we showed each other the list of items we had ranked and rewritten.

Given this achievement, I decided to introduce a new enactment involving more of Larry's body that could stimulate embodied meanings related to his rigidity and provide him the opportunity to experience sharing his rigidity. After we each shared the list of items we had rewritten, and Larry lay down on the couch, I asked him to please turn around and take a look before he starts to read his list. I placed my sheet of paper on my head. Larry sat up on the couch, turned around, and his facial expression suggested surprise. I explained that when the paper is on my head, it might help me get some ideas about what I listed. I asked Larry to place his sheet of paper under the pillow after he read each item so the list is close to his head. I added that maybe there's another list inside of him, so putting the list under the pillow might help the other list to come out. Laughing, Larry placed his paper under the pillow, "Now you're really crazy, but I guess you know what you're doing." Sometimes after placing his paper under the pillow, he would turn around, look up and ask me if I got any other ideas when I placed my paper on my head. I turned my head back and forth, indicating that I did not experience any new ideas, because I wanted Larry to experience me sharing his rigidity. During the following weeks, Larry's mood gradually became more positive as he participated in this enactment. At one point I pointed out to him that we are definitely walking side by side, and was sure that someday we will find a way that will make the lists we bring to our sessions come up with other ideas.

Because the microbody enactment involving having a sheet of paper near your head contributed to Larry and I continuing to cultivate a shared interactive language and reciprocal relationship, and also gave Larry the opportunity to experience me sharing his rigidity, I decided to try an enactment that would engage all of Larry's body and represent rigidity that we would also share. At the start of our fifth month, before Larry arrived, I lowered the window shades hanging from each of the six windows in my office, so that they were all uneven. For example, I adjusted one so that it was about two feet from the window sill, and another about three inches from the window sill. When Larry arrived and walked toward the couch, I commented, "Excuse me Larry. Before you get started, I would appreciate it if you would watch me do something for a minute, and then maybe you can help me. I'm sure you noticed that the window shades are not even." I pointed to the window shade that was hanging three inches from the window sill. "See, this shade is almost all the way down so nothing from the outside can come in, and nothing from the inside can go out." Then I pointed to the window shade that was rolled up several inches from the top. "But this shade is almost to the top, so the window is wide open, and what is outside can come in and what is inside can go out." Larry replied, "I get it." With ruler in hand I walked to the window that was rolled up near the top, reached up and slowly pulled down the window shade. Then I carefully measured the distance from the bottom of the shade to the window sill to ensure the distance was exactly four inches. I turned to Larry, "See. Now this shade keeps most of what's outside from coming in and what's inside from going out. Just a little bit can go in and out." I stepped to another window, "Here's another one that needs to be fixed. " I pulled down the shade and carefully measured the distance between the shade and the sill, stood up and turned to Larry. "What do you think? Please join me in this game for a few minutes and check to see if these other widow shades are exactly four inches from the window sill." Chuckling, Larry walked over, "You're still crazy, but I still trust that you know what you are doing." Smiling, I handed Larry the ruler. "Thanks. Please check the window shades I just fixed." Larry took the ruler and carefully measured each shade. Smiling, he commented, "This one is great, but this one is a half inch off." (I had intentionally made the error.) I joined Larry's humorous tone, "Larry, let's make this the window game. What if we take a few minutes at the start of each session, and you fix and measure three window shades, and I fix and measure the other three. Then you check what I did, and I check what you did to see who wins the window game that day." During the next weeks, Larry and I participated in the "window game" for about ten minutes at the start of each of the following sessions. I intentionally made sure that one of my shades was about a half inch off. Larry cheered and laughed each time he discovered and corrected my error. Also, Larry kept score and clearly was enjoying the game.

Given Larry's positive participation and happy tone as he interacted with me in this enactment, I decided to modify the enactment, step by step, each providing an embodied experience representing a gradual increase in flexibility. When Larry entered the office, he asked for the ruler. As he walked toward a window, I asked him to please consider an idea I got about our game, after we met last Friday. I suggested that now we lower the window shade six inches from the window sill, instead of four inches, "so that a little bit more from the inside can go outside and a little bit more from the outside can go inside." Larry replied, "Great. That's OK with me." During this and the next three sessions, the window game focused on an opening of six inches. From this point on, in order "to let more from the inside go out and more from the outside go in," during each of four sessions of the following weeks, the window game involved measuring the shades twelve inches from the sill, then eighteen inches, then twenty four inches, then thirty.

I was pleased to notice that during these weeks while on the couch, Larry gradually expressed himself in a less regimented way and occasionally associated spontaneously to an incident he described. For example during one session, an item on his list concerned how again he wanted to get up during a meeting the director of his unit was holding, minutes before the meeting was over. After reading the item, Larry shared, "I don't know why but this time, before I stood up, I was focused on whether I was sitting the right way in my chair. Like, if I wasn't sitting right, I couldn't do my job right." Larry had nothing else to share about his preoccupation with how he was sitting in his chair. However, the meaning of this association related to traumatic, childhood experiences that were revealed later.

Because Larry had responded in a positive way while gradually raising window shades higher, and because his cognitive-emotional flow seemed less regimented, I decided to initiate a very different enactment to explore whether it would contribute to modifying his rigid cognitive-emotional orientation and instrumental behavior and promote flexibility between his I-Self and Me-Self. At the start of a session, after each of us had measured our window shades at the distance of thirty inches, I commented that since we were allowing much more from the inside to go out and more from the outside to go in, I thought of another window game. "We can call the game flying free. Now everything inside can go out and everything outside can go in. Watch, here's the game." I carefully pulled down one of the shades until my hand was near the window sill, and then released the shade so that it quickly snapped and rolled upward to the top. I turned to Larry, "See, because the shade can fly free, now whatever is inside is free to go out and whatever is outside is free to come in. Try one, Larry, and see what you think about this new game." Again Larry joked that I was crazy. He slowly walked to a window and took hold of a shade. I noticed that now his emotional tone was tense and different than the happy mood and invested attention he had expressed when measuring the distance of each shade from the window sill. I commented, "Larry, I know this part of the game seems crazy. See if you can make that shade snap up and fly free." Larry took hold of the shade, pulled it down a little, released it and lifted his head, watching the shade roll upwards." Wow that's not easy, but I will try to fly more free than you." I commented, "Great. Let's keep doing this and see if it's fun to fly free." As we repeated this enactment at the start of the next several sessions, Larry's sense of pleasure increased. Frequently he shouted, "Now I fly free!"

Because of his positive response, in one session I introduced another enactment in an effort to extend the embodied meaning of flying free into the outer world. I asked him to step over to a table on which I had placed two quart bottles of water next to a bucket. I commented that the water in each bottle feels "very contained," and would also like to flow free just like water in a river. I added that each of us take a bottle, remove the cork from the bottle, and help the water flow free into the pan. Initially Larry carefully tilted the bottle and dribbled the water into the bucket. Each time we repeated this, I poured my bottle a little more vigorously than did Larry. After we engaged this enactment for several sessions, he imitated me, quickly tipping the bottle over so that the water poured into the pan. At one point I was very pleased when Larry exclaimed with a smile after pouring water from his bottle, "Wow, now it's really free to flow down the river. Whatever is inside can go outside!" His comment indicated that the embodied meaning he experienced when measuring window shades was being integrated with the embodied meaning stimulated by pouring water. Larry and I repeated these enactments at the start of each session for two weeks. First we played having the shades fly free, and then we played having the water flow free down the river. During these sessions, for the first time, Larry expressed opinions about my body. While lying on the couch, he lifted himself up with his elbows, turned his head, looked back at me and commented, "You're not sitting in your chair like you usually do." In response, I shifted myself in my chair and asked, "How about now, is this OK?" The clinical relevance of Larry commenting about the way I was sitting was clarified three sessions later.

When Larry entered the office at the start of this session, he held his hands up and commented, "See, I did not make a list for today, but I have something very important that I want to talk about. Can we please do that instead of playing the fly free game and the water game? " I noticed that Larry seemed very anxious, wondered whether a tragedy happened, and replied that I really wanted to know what he wants to share. He flopped on the couch and exclaimed, "Last night I woke up from a terrible nightmare." While pushing his arms up and down he elaborated with much anxiety, "I kept falling through black space, and I kept throwing my arms out, hoping I could grab something to stop me from falling. But I kept falling though this black space!" Because he seemed to be experiencing a panic attack, I leaned forward, reached out, grabbed one of his hands, held it and commented, "Gee, Larry that must have been really scary. I know we can figure it out." Larry replied, "Thanks a lot," and gradually became more relaxed. I thought that Larry now displayed some evidence that his I-Self and Me-Self had been connected to some degree. Given this impression, for a moment I asked Larry to associate to the nightmare. "Larry, like I said, I know that the nightmare you had was very scary. But let's take a minute to see if the picture of you falling through black space makes you think about anything." Larry closed his eyes, remained silent for several minutes and replied with a tone of emphasis, "No nothing." During the remaining minutes, he discussed assignments he was given at his office.

In the next session, Larry demonstrated that the door that had been shut tight, blocking the calls for action from embodied meanings representing early traumatic experiences, was now unlocked. Larry again did not arrive with a list. After playing the "fly free" game and the "water flow free" game for a few minutes, he got on the couch and noted that although he is still struggling with the nightmare, something happened at work early this morning that got him upset and that he wants to talk about. Expressing genuine concern, I mentioned that I was very eager to learn what happened. Larry shared the following. When Larry walked into the conference room at the start of a meeting, the head of the department commented, "Larry I always bug you, but today we have several important things to handle, so please remain in your seat until we're finished." After Larry described the incident, with a tone of investment I replied, "Larry, I know this issue also came up a couple of times weeks ago. Now I think it could teach us something. Try to picture yourself sitting in that chair with the department head nearby, and see if makes you think of anything." Larry's response pleased me because it illustrated that the enactments in which we had participated cultivated some flexibility in his cognitive-emotional orientation and had connected his I-Self and Me-Self. He did not respond as he had yesterday. Instead Larry exclaimed, "This sounds crazy, but the first thing that flashed into my mind is that nightmare of me falling through black space. But a second later I got another flashback that I'm falling down a huge pipe, like I'm being flushed." I replied, "Wow Larry, you're helping us a lot. Now take a minute and see if flushing down a pipe makes you think of anything." Larry shouted, "Oh my God! I just remembered something that always happened when I was a little kid."

Larry shared the following. From the time he began using the toilet, his mother required him to remain seated on the toilet until he had a bowel movement, and urged him to count the stools each time because it would show if he is eating healthy. She also required him to call her when he was "finished," and before he flushed the toilet, so that she could "check that all was OK." Larry added that once in a while he would leave the bathroom without calling his mother, because he could not "perform." When his mother "checked" and discovered that he was no longer in the bathroom, she looked for him and spanked him. During the following sessions, Larry continued recalling and sharing experiences he had with his mother most of which were traumatic. For example, when he started kindergarten his mother assigned him a "job." He was to place napkins exactly three inches from the plates at dinnertime, and also place silverware in positions she designated. Similarly, she "taught" him to place his socks and underwear in particular drawers and place toys in specific boxes. Sometimes if he placed a toy in the wrong box, she would get angry and slap him and exclaimed, "I'm teaching you how to be organized!"

During one session, Larry spontaneously shared experiences that involved his father. For example, while expressing frustration Larry recalled that his father, "was always doing some office stuff or reading the newspaper" when at home, and rarely engaged him in games. At one point while discussing his father Larry commented, "Remember a couple of weeks ago when I first told you about the nightmare, you reached out and held my hand. Well my father never held my hand that I could remember." I thanked Larry and asked him to get up from the couch and join me for a minute so we can experience something together. I pointed out that since the nightmare, what he has been sharing for a number of sessions illustrates that now what is outside is free to fly in and what is inside is free to fly out. Given that accomplishment, I suggested that we experience outside together. He chuckled and commented that he would love to do that. We walked outside. The building in which my office was located was one of many buildings of an inpatient psychiatric hospital. Larry walked about feeling the breeze on his face and body and touching the leaves of a nearby bush. At one point I asked him to look up at a large tree that shows how tall his self has grown. Larry smiled, looked up at the tree and exclaimed; "Now I feel my arms are around the outside world!" As we walked about, Larry scanned the landscape that surrounded the buildings and noticed horseshoes on the ground next to a stake. Laughing, he asked, "Why are those here?" I explained that it was for patients in the hospital who might want to go outside with a staff member and engage in something that was fun. Larry noted that since we played games with window shades and water bottles, now he would like to play a horseshoe game. I was delighted with his request and agreed. We tossed horseshoes for about ten minutes with much joking. When we returned to the office, Larry asked if we could play horseshoes for a few minutes before the next sessions like we used to play the window shade and water games. With much excitement I agreed. We started each of the next several sessions joking and enjoying playing horseshoes for ten minutes.

During the next several weeks, Larry continued sharing traumatic experiences with his mother and father with much emotion. At times I interpreted these experiences and related them to particular aspects of his behavior, because Larry seemed ready to understand, at the verbal and conscious level, what he had been expressing with his rigid nonverbal behavior. The following are examples: (A) Keeping a list of items related to his mother requiring him to keep track of how many stools he produced; (B) Measuring napkins and silverware before dinnertime, behavior that upset his wife, came from his mother requiring him to put napkins exactly three inches from the plates and counting his stools; (C) At the company where he worked, leaving meetings before they were over related to his wanting to leave the bathroom and escape from his mother; (D) His difficulty interacting playfully with his children related to his having no playful experiences with his father or mother.

Larry was receptive to the interpretations I offered and shared related experiences, continuing to illustrate that he had developed flexibility between his I-Self and Me-Self, and also among embodied meanings, cognitive-emotional orientation, instrumental-expressive behaviors and the calls for action from environments. For example, he shared that his wife recently told him that she now feels much happier because recently he has spontaneously helped doing things like emptying the dishwasher and folding laundry, and that he no longer checks the napkins that the children put on the table by the dishes. Regarding his children, he shared that he is beginning to enjoy interacting and playing with them and now goes outside with them and plays different games. He noted that one of the games he plays with his son is horseshoes. Laughing he commented, "I'm helping him be as good as you are flipping those horseshoes." At the accounting firm, the young man whom he supervises, and who said months ago, "We're not connected" recently commented, "Larry now I feel we're a team." At one point Larry reviewed aspects of his history, and when I commented, "I feel really sorry about all of what you had to put up with," he replied, "You saved my life."

Concluding Comment

Larry's traumatic childhood experiences interfered to a significant degree with his psychological development and were the source of his developing a very rigid outer cognitive-emotional orientation, expressed in very rigid instrumental-expressive behaviors, that enabled him to keep these past traumatic experiences behind a closed door, while he occupied himself with external events (e.g., the location of napkins, keeping a list of what to do each day). This cognitive and behavioral rigidity interfered with his relationships and interactions with his wife, children and fellow workers. It seems clear that engaging Larry only in talk therapy would not have helped. In the first phase of enactments (measuring window shades to insure they are close to the window sill) engaged Larry in body experiences replicating and symbolizing the embodied meaning of his rigid, outer cognitive-emotional orientation and instrumental-expressive behavior, namely that what is inside cannot go out. Then engaging him in a series of enactments that replicated embodied meanings representing a gradual increase in flexibility between the I-Self and Me-Self provided him with the opportunity to experience new embodied meanings that promoted flexibility in his cognitive-emotional orientation and instrumental-expressive behavior, and enabled him to construct insights: (A) Repeating the enactment of gradually raising and measuring window shades a small distance provided body experiences and embodied meaning representing what is inside can gradually go outside and what is outside can gradually go inside; (B) Repeating the enactments of flipping up window shades, and pouring water out of a bottle, provided body experiences and embodied meaning representing that all of what is inside is free to go outside and all that is outside is free to go inside. This sequence of enactments established a link between Larry's I-Self and Me-Self, and eventually resulted in Larry experiencing a nightmare about falling in black space and down a huge pipe. Also, because the enactments cultivated reflexivity, the capacity to experience, observe, and reflect on oneself as both subject and object (noted by Aron at the start of this chapter), Larry was now able to free associate to the nightmare and recall memories. The process of enactments contributed to Larry resolving the trauma he had endured and developing a new self that was now capable of improving his relationships and interactions with family members and persons in his work environment.

THERAPY CASE 2

ALICE: A VERY RIGID OUTER COGNITIVE-EMOTIONAL ORIENTATION AND RIGID INSTRUMENTAL-EXPRESSIVE BEHAVIOR

Alice, who had just turned fifteen years old and started her sophomore year in high school, was referred by her parents at the urging of the school principal and guidance counselor. Her parents shared the following at our first meeting. During her freshman year, Alice had been referred by her teachers to a guidance counselor several times because she related to them with a very angry tone, and sometimes did not complete her work adequately. Alice met with a guidance counselor throughout the school year. In spite of the help she received, she continued this angry behavior at the start of her sophomore year. However, now her anger was focused on her homeroom teacher. A recent episode promoted the referral. While this teacher was talking to a student, Alice stood nearby waiting to address the teacher. Suddenly Alice rushed forward and screamed at the teacher, "When do you care about me?" The parents acknowledged that Alice had shown similar angry behavior with teachers throughout her grade-school years, but not with her mother. The parents also discussed that Alice has been a binge eater. At breakfast, but more often at dinner-time, she comments that she is not hungry and does not want to eat. She then goes to her bedroom and "stuffs a lot of food into herself" that she apparently had collected.

Her parents also shared the following history and "guessed" that it probably relates to Alice's difficulties. Mother became pregnant after Alice turned two years old, and a baby girl, Nancy, was born shortly after Alice reached her third birthday. But Nancy died two months later because of "physical complications." Mother became very depressed, left home for four months to be with her parents, and a nanny was hired to care for Alice. When I asked what they could recall about Alice's behavior during that period of time, mother focused on the following. After mother became pregnant, and the fetus grew larger, Alice initiated play rituals. With one, she would sit next to mother, tapped mother's stomach and called out to the fetus, "I want to play with you." With the other, whenever Mom got into bed to rest during the afternoon, Alice would lie across mother's belly laughing, "I'm the baby." I inquired about Alice's behavior when Nancy died and mother left for several months. Father commented, "For me Alice seemed tuned out, and she would get mad about different things." Mother interrupted, asking her husband to recall that when she returned, the nanny did not report that there had been any problems with Alice. Mother acknowledged, however, that she continued to be depressed for several years and was not "very involved" with Alice.

I began working with Alice twice a week and experienced her as very bright and verbally articulate. During our first meetings I mentioned to her that, as she knew I had met with her parents but I would appreciate it very much if she would share with me in what way she thinks I could be of help. Alice did not respond and continued to express anger about her homeroom teacher, Miss Green, who also teaches her social studies class. I asked, "What does Miss Green do that makes you so angry?" With much anger Alice described several details about Miss Green; for example, her facial expressions; the way she talks, gestures, and walks; the clothes she wears. While sharing these details, Alice shouted, "She's always interested in other students!" When I asked Alice to share what she thinks about other teachers, she made neutral comments and then immediately returned to blasting Miss Green. Also, because I noticed that she was complaining about a female teacher, I asked her if she had any male teachers. She replied, "My science teacher and math teacher are guys." When I asked her to share what they are like, she replied, "They're OK," and again immediately returned to complaining about Miss Green. On two occasions as Alice complained about what Miss Green was wearing or the way she talked, I asked her if what she just shared reminded her of anything. She responded, "No," continued blasting Miss Green and elaborated her complaints. Whenever I asked about her meeting with the guidance counselor, her typical response was, "This is what I hated. She kept saying I'm probably mad at somebody else, because Miss Green is a nice person."

During our fourth meeting, because Alice continued blasting Miss Green and repeated her complaints, I found it difficult to keep my attention focused on Alice, and once in a while glanced at the book shelves on either side of her. At one moment Alice got angry with me, "You did it again! You're not looking at me." I apologized, shared that I am hearing everything she is saying and will try to keep looking at her. Alice's behavior during these first sessions, as well as the history her parents shared, contributed to the opinion I had already developed. Because of early developmental interferences related to her mother's absence for four months, and her depression for several years, and Nancy's death, I thought that Alice must have developed a very rigid outer cognitive-emotional orientation and rigid instrumental-expressive behavior displayed by her constantly complaining about her teachers during her grade-school years. Now Alice's rigidity focused on yelling about Miss Green. This outer orientation and rigid behavior may be helping her to avoid embodied meanings related to trauma she had experienced. I set this opinion to one side and decided to explore during the next sessions whether Alice could free associate. For example, after she described with anger and in detail what Miss Green was wearing, I responded, "Alice please close your eyes and keep looking at that picture of Miss Green in your mind and see if it makes you think of anything else." Alice never responded with an association, and usually replied, "It just reminds me of that bitch." During one of these sessions, my countertransference and frustration, related to my struggling with her constantly screaming about Miss Green, must have influenced my tone and the way I expressed myself. After Alice again complained about Miss Green, I commented, "Alice, now we have another reason to be mad at her." Alice replied, "See, did you notice the way you said that? You must still be mad at me. Last week you didn't look at me, now you sound irritated." My response at this moment was influenced by the following. After the previous two sessions, I had given a lot of thought to the type of enactments I could introduce that might contribute to Alice and I cultivating a shared interactive language and that would launch a process cultivating her ability to experience embodied meanings. I commented, "Alice, I'm really sorry. You're right. The way I said that was not the way I usually talk to you. I'm frustrated and all tangled up trying to find a way to join you." I explained that I had an idea about a game she and I could play. After Alice describes some detail about Miss Green, we take turns and yell for one minute, and Alice decides who wins. Alice apparently experienced my apology as sincere and responded with excitement. In this session, and at the start of the next several sessions, we played the yelling game. Alice commented several times that I was "doing a really good job."

Given that we had cultivated the beginning of a shared interactive language, at the start of one session I commented, "Alice, guess what. I figured out another game we could play and see who wins." Alice responded with excitement, "What's the game?" Influenced by my research using the Two-Person Drawing Test described in chapter 2, I handed Alice a sheet of paper and a pencil and asked her to draw a picture of Miss Green doing something. I explained we would use the picture in a game where we compete. Alice grinned, grabbed the paper and pencil and drew a picture of a woman with arms raised. When she finished, she exclaimed, "OK what's the game?" I tapped the picture on a nearby wall, explained that each of us would take turns yelling at the picture, and Alice would decide who wins each round and keeps score. Alice leaped up and declared that I go first. I stood about two feet from the picture and yelled for about fifteen seconds, trying my best to imitate Alice's body rhythm, gestures, and tone. I exclaimed for example, "You are the biggest jerk ever! Look at the stupid dress you're wearing!" Alice then screamed at the picture and declared she won. We played the game six more times. Alice exclaimed that she "loved the game" and declared she won four of the games. At the start of the next several sessions we participated in this enactment. In the third session of this series, Alice asked me to draw a picture of Miss Green that we could yell at. In the following sessions we took turns drawing a picture and pasting it on the wall. While shouting, I intentionally leaned forward, toward the picture, a little at a time, so that at one point during this series of sessions my nose was several inches away from the picture. Alice must have observed my enactment because she began leaning toward the picture so that at one point her nose was almost touching the paper. I was pleased that Alice and I took turns drawing a picture of Miss Green, and that Alice was imitating me leaning forward while yelling, because these developments reflected that Alice was joining me cultivating a shared interactive language. In each session after playing the yelling game, Alice continued her diatribe about Miss Green.

When I noticed that her body was imitating my body leaning closer to the picture, I decided to initiate another enactment that included an instrumental-expressive action at the microbody level. My goal was to explore whether the enactment would cultivate some flexibility in Alice's I-Self that constantly used the verbal mode (screaming about Miss Green). At the start of one session before taping a picture on the wall, I shared with Alice that I had thought of another way we could compete that would give us a break from yelling. Alice smiled, "OK. Now what game did you cook up." I explained that with this new game she draws a picture of Miss Green doing something on each of two sheets of paper. I placed two sheets of paper on the small table next to her chair and explained that after she completes the drawings, I tear my sheet in half as fast as I can, and then she tears her sheet as fast as possible. I added that every time we play the game she decides who tore with the most power and keeps score. Alice smiled, "Great!" Alice took the pencil on her table and with vigor sketched the outline of a person on each sheet of paper and shouted, "That's Miss Green teaching the class again! Now we can tear her apart!" I took hold of one sheet of paper, raised my arms and ripped the sheet in half. Alice smiled, picked up the other sheet of paper, carefully placed the fingers of both hands at the top and center of the paper, slowly raised her arms, and vigorously ripped the paper in half. Alice screamed, "Wow, I really tore her apart." Laughing, I commented that I agreed because she really crushed her sheet of paper. I handed Alice a small pad, noted that it would be great if she kept a record of the "Tear Hard" game, and asked her to record who won today. Smiling and with much pleasure, Alice commented, "Sorry for you, I won," took the pad and scribbled on the page. Joining her tone I smiled and commented, "Absolutely, you did win Alice. But let's see who wins the next time we meet." We played the "Tear Hard" game at the start of the next eight sessions, and Alice continued to tear the sheet of paper with much vigor and cheered with excitement as she won each time. During each of these sessions whenever Alice screamed about Miss Green, I interrupted her diatribe, "Alice, why don't we play the Tear Hard game and then you can tear her apart." Each time Alice yelled, "Fantastic!" smiled while sketching a picture of Miss Green on each sheet of paper, and played the game with much vigor. Her very positive response each time we played the Tear Hard game indicated that a degree of flexibility in her cognitive-emotional orientation and instrumental-expressive behavior was developing. Her Me-Self was now experiencing the embodied meaning expressed by the fantasy that Miss Green is the drawing on a sheet of paper, and her I-Self was interpreting that tearing the sheet of paper is a symbolic expression of anger toward Miss Green.

During the ninth session of this phase because of the flexibility Alice was displaying, I decided to introduce another enactment to explore if the flexibility could be extended into and negotiated with the external environment. After playing the Tear Hard game twice, I stood up and commented that I had an idea about another game we could play that had to do with yelling about Miss Green. I commented. "Alice, like when you just tore the paper, you yelled she's a jerk!" I was pleased that Alice noticed the way I imitated her which I frequently did in order to continue developing a shared interactive language. Alice asked, "Great. What's the game?" I stepped toward one of the windows in the office. "Please come over here and look out the window at this huge tree." My office was now on the second floor of a building located in a residential community, and a very large therapeutic garden (Santostefano, 2004) had been constructed surrounding this building. Alice stepped next to me and looked out the window. I pointed, "See that huge tree right by that little hill. Let's pretend that tree is Miss Green standing there and teaching those bushes. My game is we yell at the tree and see who yells the best." Alice exclaimed, "Fantastic, that's a great game too! You go first, so I can see how loud I should yell." I stood before the window, leaned forward and yelled, "You jerk!" I turned to Alice, "Please tell me if I did a good job letting Miss Green know what a jerk she is." Alice replied, "That was good." She stepped before the window, leaned forward so that her nose was an inch or two from the window, and screamed, "You're the biggest jerk in the world!" Alice decided she had yelled the best, and I agreed. At the start of the next five sessions, we played the "Yelling at the Tree Game" after playing the Tear Hard game.

At this point I decided to introduce another enactment to explore whether the body experience, and the meaning it stimulated, could also contribute to Alice regulating her anger and expressing other behaviors, instead of the rigid behavior of yelling about Miss Green. I also introduced the new enactment to explore whether the body experience might stimulate other meanings. At the start of the next session I commented that instead of playing the Tear Hard game before we play the Yelling at the Tree Game I had thought of another one. Again she commented with interest and wondered what the game was about. I responded that I look forward to her sharing if she thinks the new game is good enough to play. Before Alice arrived, I had placed sheets of paper on the small table near my chair. I picked up one of the sheets and held it up and explained that the game had to do with who can tear a sheet of paper the slowest. I handed Alice a stop watch and asked her to measure how much time I take to tear it. Alice looked at the stopwatch, paused and whispered, "Ready, go." With much drama I slowly tore the paper in half and asked Alice how much time I took. Alice grinned, "Fifteen seconds." I also grinned, and asked Alice if she thought she could do better. Now Alice chuckled, "Yes, and get ready to lose." Alice handed me the stopwatch, picked up a sheet of paper, held it high and began to slowly tear it in half. I was impressed by how involved she seemed to be in this enactment. "How did I do?" I smiled and informed her that she won again with a time of twenty five seconds. Alice laughed, "Well I bet that I will reach a minute. Let's play this again." I slowly tore another sheet of paper, and Alice announced that I had achieved twenty seconds. When Alice took her turn, she had become so involved in tearing the paper slowly that she achieved thirty seconds. She exclaimed with pride, "I won again!" We played the Yelling at the Tree Game and the Tear Slowly game during the next seven sessions.

At the start of the following session Alice decided that we would no longer play Yelling at the Tree game. During this and the following sessions she displayed behaviors different from those of the past. Sometimes she discussed Miss Green, but unlike past meetings, she did not occupy herself during the whole session with this topic, nor did she express the intense anger she typically had. For example, occasionally she commented about a classmate and a weekend trip she and her parents were planning to take to Maine. Also during these sessions, Alice occasionally performed a gesture she had never displayed before that involved her body. While talking, she slowly moved the palm of her hand in a circular motion over her stomach for about a minute. Although I did not understand the meaning of this gesture, I slowly moved the palm of my hand over my stomach a couple of times to continue negotiating a shared interactive language. Whenever Alice performed this gesture, I wondered whether its meaning related to the issue of nurture and her binge eating. She repeated this gesture during the next several sessions which pleased me because it suggested that Alice was not rigidly focused on Miss Green and that her body was beginning to speak. I continued to occasionally imitate her gesture. Three sessions later her body elaborated the meaning that was developing. When we walked into the office at the start of a session, Alice pointed to the analysis couch. "That's where some patients lie down, right? They talk about things to get help." I replied she was correct and was impressed because from the time Alice and I began meeting, the couch had always been there, but she had never made a comment about it. Alice added, "My parents told me that when I asked them the other day what the couch was about." She paused, stared at the couch and commented that she has an idea about a new game. "Watch this." Alice walked across the room and playfully flopped on the couch. "You sit there while I'm on the couch." She remained on the couch for several minutes and continued her discussion, while holding a pillow on her stomach. Several times she commented, "This feels good." I asked her what about what she is doing feels good, but she did not respond and continued her discussion. Alice repeated this behavior at the start of the next two sessions.

To continue negotiating a shared interactive language and encourage Alice's body to continue speaking, at the start of the next session I introduced an enactment that was influenced by Alice's enactment. After Alice flopped on the couch for several minutes and then stood up, I commented, "Alice, I'm joining your game, but I'm adding something so you and I can start a new kind of therapy." I playfully flopped on the couch. "See, now the therapist lies on the couch and the patient sits in the chair behind the couch." Alice burst out laughing. "OK but in this new therapy, the therapist has to hold a pillow on his stomach." I joined the laughter and placed a pillow on my stomach. Given that she had held a pillow on her stomach each time she was on the couch, to explore what the pillow represented, I placed my hands on the pillow and commented, "Wow, I think I got fat. I wonder why?" Alice laughed, "No you're not fat. So what do you want to talk about for a minute?" I replied that because I still want to help her, even though the therapist is on the couch, in this new therapy the patient can talk about whatever she wants while sitting on the chair. Alice laughed and began discussing homework she had to do. While she discussed details, the pillow on my stomach must have moved to the side. Alice laughed, "In this new therapy the pillow has to stay at the very top of your stomach."

We played the "New Therapy Game" at the start of the next several sessions. In one session after playing this game, Alice initiated another activity that impressed me because it added to my opinion that, from the time we played the Tear Hard game, then the Tear Slowly game, the Yelling at the Tree game, and the New Therapy game, Miss Green was mentioned once or twice during the session. Also, embodied meanings were being expressed and elaborated. When she got up from the couch, she commented, "Remember when we played the game of yelling at the tree. Can we go outside for a few minutes and walk around that little hill by the tree we yelled at." I replied with a very positive tone, and she led us into the therapeutic garden. For several minutes she slowly walked about, sometimes touching bushes. Then she walked to the top of a mount and sat down. I sat next to her. While looking about she commented several times in a soft tone, "This is nice. I really like it here." She remained on the mount for the rest of the session and talked about her experiences at school. Again, Miss Green was the target of a complaint only once. During the next four sessions, she elected to go outside and climbed to the top of the mount. I noticed that now during each session, she remained seated for several minutes, then stretched out over the mount in a prone position for several minutes, and then sat down. She repeated this several times. Whether she was sitting down or lying down, I sat next to her and participated in her discussions.

After repeating sitting and lying on the mount for five sessions, her body announced that its door that had been locked for years was now totally open so that all embodied meanings could speak out. While stretched out in a prone position over the mount, Alice interrupted her discussion of events at school and commented with a tone that expressed concern, "I just got a very weird feeling." I asked Alice to help me understand what she meant by "weird." She replied, "I can't because the feeling is too embarrassing" and remained silent. In an effort to convey that I was very invested in helping her at this moment, and was trying to experience what she was experiencing, I stretched out in a prone position two feet from her. She remained silent for many minutes, and I made a couple of comments. For example, I noted that it does feel kind of weird and we will eventually learn what we mean by a weird feeling. Several minutes before the end of the session, Alice finally spoke up. "It feels weird because lying over this little hill feels like I'm lying on the belly of a pregnant mother." During the next five sessions, Alice continued to lie prone on the top of the mount, and I lay down in a prone position or sat next to her. Gradually she shared embodied memories that her parents had discussed with me before Alice and I started therapy. Alice recalled that when her mother would lay in bed to rest, she sometimes would stretch across her mother's belly and pretend she was the baby. She also recalled experiences that occurred during the following years: for example, after the baby died, her mother left; when her mother returned she was always "very sad;" when Alice went to preschool, her mother never became "involved."

The memories Alice was experiencing and sharing illustrated that her I-Self and Me-Self were now connected and that her cognitive-emotional orientation was now more flexible, allowing embodied meanings-emotions to contribute to how the outer world is viewed and experienced. Because of this development, I initiated an enactment that would involve her whole body and could contribute to her continuing to develop I-Self and Me-Self reflexivity and modify her rigid instrumental-expressive behavior. In one session after Alice shared some memories, I commented that I have an idea about another game and would appreciate her opinion. I explained that we could pretend the large tree is Miss Green. Instead of yelling at it like we used to, we could throw rocks at it to see who scores the most hits. I wondered to myself if we threw rocks instead of yelling, would Alice eventually modify who the large tree represented. Alice jumped up and looked for rocks. Then we stood at the top of the mount and took turns throwing a rock at the big tree. At the start of the next session, Alice immediately decided that we play the "Rock Throwing" game and introduced very significant elaborations, indicating that she was now experiencing, at the conscious level, traumatic embodied meanings that had been locked in her unconscious and the source of expressing her anger with the rigid instrumental-expressive behavior of constantly complaining about teachers, most recently Miss Green. While we stood on the top of the mount, Alice pointed to the large tree, "We used to call that tree Miss Green, but today we're calling that tree the Mother Tree." Then she pointed at the small tree, "I'm calling that the Sister Tree." Alice threw a rock at the large tree, yelling. "You left me you jerk, and you took away my sister, Nancy!" Then she hurled a rock at the small tree and yelled, "You shouldn't have died!" Alice asked me to join her and I participated with vigor. Hurling a rock at the large tree, I shouted, "You shouldn't have left Alice for so long!" When hurling a rock at the small tree I shouted, "Sorry that you died, but you shouldn't have died." Alice continued to keep a record of who hit the trees most often.

After devoting three sessions to the Rock Throwing game, Alice introduced another activity related to her binge eating, an issue that had not yet entered our relationship. In one session after throwing rocks, she turned to me. "I feel a little hungry. Could I have a snack?" I responded "Of course" and asked her what she might like to eat. She replied, "I like peanut butter crackers, if you have them." I ran to the clinic's kitchen, obtained a box of peanut butter crackers and a bottle of orange juice, rushed back to the mount, and handed them to Alice. She sat down and vigorously gulped down crackers. During the next session, after throwing rocks at the trees, she again gulped crackers. In the following session, anticipating that she would continue asking for food, when she arrived I invited her to come with me to the kitchen and prepare what she would like to eat. Alice seemed pleased, accompanied me to the kitchen, and carefully examined what was in the refrigerator and the pantry. However, she picked up a box of peanut butter crackers, took it outside, and vigorously gulped down several crackers while sitting on the mount.

At the start of the next session, given the progress Alice had made, I introduced an enactment in an effort to deal with the binge eating. After we threw rocks, Alice asked for a snack, and we obtained another box of peanut butter crackers. While we sat on the mount, I commented that I would love it if we have a "Snack Game," and she asked me to describe the game. I asked her to recall the game when we tore a sheet of paper as slowly as possible and timed each other with a stopwatch to see who won. I handed her the stop watch and asked her to put a cracker in my mouth. I chewed it, exaggerating a very slow motion. After I swallowed the cracker, I asked Alice, "How did I do?" Grinning, she replied, "Forty-three seconds." I announced it was her turn, I bet she will not beat me, and placed a cracker in her mouth. She chewed with some vigor, but not as she had in the previous sessions. When she finished chewing and swallowed the cracker, I looked at the stopwatch and commented that her score was twenty seconds. Alice responded, "I know you won. I have to really work on that." We repeated this enactment during the next six sessions. After each enactment, Alice continued eating crackers while we discussed various issues. I was pleased to observe that not only did Alice's chewing gradually become slower, but especially that she gradually decreased the number of crackers she ate after each enactment.

In the last phase of our work, Alice and I participated in another enactment. In one session while walking about the therapeutic garden, Alice pointed at a tall evergreen tree and commented that she would like to call it, "'Mom,' because it is really nice." I asked her if there was one we could call "Nancy." Because there were no small evergreen trees nearby, Alice expressed disappointment. I suggested that I could obtain a small one, and the next time we meet, we could plant it by the Mom tree.

I obtained a very small evergreen, and with much feeling Alice decided exactly where we would locate it. She joined me digging the site she had designated and planting the tree. When we finished, she pointed at the small tree and commented, "Now Nancy can keep growing up." Alice added that as she continues high school, she will ask her parents to take her here once in a while so she can "watch Nancy growing up and see how she's doing." She added, "Then when I come to see Nancy, it will give me a chance to visit you for a minute." I responded, "That would be great!" Also, during the final minutes of our last session, Alice commented, "There's something I want to ask you." She stood up and walked over to a basket of small stones, noting that she has always glanced at the stones when she entered the office. Smiling she commented, "They are really nice." She asked me where I found the stones, and I explained that I had brought them from a village in Sicily, whenever I went there to visit my relatives. Alice asked if she could have one, and I replied "Absolutely." She carefully examined the collection, selected one, and thanked me with much feeling. She held the stone in her hand when she left.

Concluding Comments

During the last phase of my work with Alice, her parents informed me that Alice had been joining them for dinner, and no longer declares she is not hungry and does not go to her room to binge eat. Also they were pleased that during dinner she now seemed relaxed and spontaneously shared experiences at school. In addition, the school counselor reported to the parents that Alice's insolent, angry attitude had gradually decreased throughout her sophomore year, and her junior year teachers were impressed that she chatted with them on occasion and had cultivated friendships with fellow students. The series of enactments in which Alice and I participated provided her with the opportunity to experience, express, and gradually revise embodied meanings representing the emotional trauma and developmental interferences she had endured. These included yelling at a drawing of Miss Green; tearing a sheet of paper on which was a drawing of Miss Green as fast as you can; yelling at a tree; tearing a sheet of paper as slow as possible; taking turns flopping on the couch and holding a pillow over your stomach; lying on the mount in a prone position; throwing rocks at a big tree and small tree; chewing crackers fast and then chewing crackers slowly; planting an evergreen tree. As embodied meanings were being experienced and expressed with these enactments, the reflexivity between Alice's I-Self and Me-Self increased and resulted in Alice's very rigid cognitive-emotional orientation and instrumental-expressive behavior becoming more flexible so that Miss Green was no longer the target at which Alice directed her rage.

THERAPY CASE 3

VERA: A VERY RIGID INNER COGNITIVE-EMOTIONAL ORIENTATION AND RIGID INSTRUMENTAL-EXPRESSIVE BEHAVIOR

Vera was referred for treatment at the age of five years, eight months because for the past three years she had been experiencing major difficulties at home and now in her kindergarten class.[1] Her adoptive parents understood that these difficulties related to the physical and emotional trauma she had experienced in a government-operated orphanage located in an eastern European country. The parents shared the following during my initial meeting with them. After making necessary arrangements through an international adoption agency, they traveled to the orphanage when Vera was three years old. Upon arrival they noticed that she had bruises on her head and body, and the staff explained they were due to her falling down. When they returned to their home in the United States, Vera immediately displayed major problems. At dinnertime when they placed food before her, she refused to touch the food and silverware, and sometimes tilted her head back with her mouth wide open. The parents patiently fed her and related her problem eating to recently released media reports concerning the orphanages in Vera's country of origin. The parents shared that at mealtime children were lined up in a row and required to tilt their heads back, as a staff member stepped from child to child and placed a spoonful of food into the mouth of each child. Whenever the child spontaneously reached up to the bowl, the staff member hit the child's hand with the spoon. In addition to her difficulties eating, when Vera entered her bedroom, she closed and barricaded the door with various items. The parents discovered the barricade each time they pushed the door open to check how she was doing.

A school psychologist urged the parents to arrange for Vera's evaluation and treatment. I met with the school psychologist to learn about her academic and social functioning in the kindergarten program. The school psychologist shared that throughout the year Vera had been very guarded in the classroom, had formed no friendships, and during recess always stood alone by a fence at the edge of the playground. Sometimes he and teachers wondered if she was mentally retarded or autistic. Also because of her very limited academic performance, she had been transferred to the slow-learning group.

During separate meetings, a female examiner and I conducted a psychological evaluation to assess Vera's intelligence, cognitive functioning and personality. When meeting with the female examiner or me, she repeated a behavior at the start of each session, replicating what her adoptive parents noted took place at home. Upon entering the playroom where the testing was conducted, she immediately placed chairs, pillows, and wooden blocks against the door, displaying rigid instrumental-expressive behavior symbolizing that she was avoiding the outer world and preventing it from reaching her. At the start of each session, the female examiner and I immediately joined her searching for items and placing them against the door. Perhaps because each of us assisted her with enthusiasm to construct the barricade, she eventually allowed each examiner to introduce and administer procedures. Although she engaged each procedure, when interacting with either examiner, she expressed intense anxiety and required much assistance. The following is a brief summary of the results. On the Wechsler Intelligence Test of Children Vera obtained a full scale IQ of 113 which surprised me given her withdrawn behavior. This result was very likely an underestimate since she had avoided some items. In terms of cognition, she was administered the Leveling-Sharpening Tests described in chapter 2, and her performance displayed a very rigid inner cognitive-emotional orientation to a significant degree. This inner orientation was also displayed by her performance with the Rorschach Ink Blot Test which I administered. She stared at each card for a minute or more, refused to share what the ink blot reminded her of, and sometimes declared, "I don't see anything." I interacted with her to provide support and encourage her to "make up" whatever the ink blot "looks like." With one card Vera constructed an image clearly representing a meaning related to her past traumatic experiences. "A bug. Someone stepped on it. The head is there. The front legs are there. The body is squashed."

On the basis of Vera's history and the test results, I concluded that although she displayed above-average intelligence, the physical and emotional abuse she had experienced resulted in the development of a very rigid, inner cognitive-emotional orientation that avoided interacting with others and experiencing environments The trauma she had experienced also resulted in the development of very rigid instrumental-expressive behavior (e.g., barricading the door to her room, standing still at the edge of the playground at school). This rigid, inner cognitive orientation and rigid behavior resulted in her very poor interpersonal and academic performance at school, leading some teachers to wonder if she was developmentally disabled or autistic, and was also the cause of her poor performance at home. However, her adoptive parents experienced moments with her contributing to their opinion that she was not retarded or autistic. The parents accepted my recommendation, and I began therapy with Vera three sessions per week during the spring months of her kindergarten year. Sometimes we met four sessions per week and continued therapy until she completed third grade.

During the first seven months of therapy (from the last months of kindergarten to the start of first grade), Vera repeated a behavior she had displayed during the evaluation. At the start of each session when we entered the playroom, she carefully closed the door and devoted ten or fifteen minutes to placing various items against the door. I quickly walked about, exaggerated my search for items, handed one to Vera and carefully placed others against the door. Following this ritual, she slowly walked about the playroom as if I were not present. I tried to keep some distance from her so that she would not experience me as intrusive. At one point I decided to introduce an enactment, hoping it would contribute to developing an interactive language that Vera and I could share. I picked up a toy animal, carefully looked at it, walked it on the floor for a minute or two, and returned it to the shelf. I repeated this for several sessions. In one session after barricading the door and slowly walking about the playroom, Vera initiated an activity that could have been stimulated by what I had been doing. She placed nine or ten toy animals on the floor in a single file, picked up the animal at the head of the line, and moved it forward about two inches. Then she picked up the animal that was second in line, moved it forward, and carefully set it down behind the first animal. She carefully continued this with each toy animal, in turn, so that the column of animals slowly "crept" across the floor into a box that she eventually called the "barn." She repeated this for several months. I understood that this activity resulted from her very rigid, inner cognitive-emotional orientation and rigid instrumental-expressive behavior, representing the meaning of the severe, interpersonal regimentation she had experienced during the first three years of her life. Once in a while, I knelt down next to Vera and carefully moved the toy animal that was next in line. However, she did not relate to my participation.

I found it very boring and difficult spending most of a session sitting on the floor watching her moving each toy animal forward a couple of inches at a time. Usually it took most of a session for her to move the line of animals across the floor to the barn. As I struggled with my frustration, a few times I introduced an activity that I thought would help Vera elaborate the meaning of this very rigid activity. But Vera's response each time made clear that I was making a mistake. For example, on one occasion, I picked up a toy animal in the line. Instead of moving it an inch forward, I turned it around and said to the animal immediately behind, "Hey, are you Nella?" Vera was clearly irritated with me because she shouted, "Shhh!" As another example, I crawled over to Vera, picked up a toy animal, turned it around and said to the toy animal behind me, "Hey, do you want to play?" Again Vera told me to be quiet, ignored what I had done, and continued moving each animal one inch at a time across the floor. Each time I apologized by gently stroking the toy animal I had picked up and commenting with feeling, "I'm really sorry." In an effort to repair the mistakes I had made, and continue trying to cultivate a shared interactive language, occasionally I took a ruler and measured the distance each toy animal was moved forward to insure it did not exceed two inches. For four months she continued to avoid me and the outer world, slowly moving toy animals across the floor. I worked hard not to introduce interactions that Vera would experience as major disruptions. I did not say a word or interact with the toy animals she had lined up. However, throughout each session I remained by her side, and joined her slowly moving each toy animal, in turn, across the floor to the barn. Very likely because I remained by her side, at one point her behavior acknowledged that I was present and being accepted. Now after she had moved a toy animal forward, and I measured the distance, she paused, looked at me and then at the next toy animal. I understood this gesture to mean it was my turn, so I imitated Vera moving it forward. Once in a while, at the start of a session Vera added a toy animal to the line. Eventually she and I slowly and carefully moved a column of thirty-four toy animals across the floor.

During the fifth month of this phase of the treatment, Vera introduced a new activity that very likely was facilitated by her experiencing me by her side for many hours, invested in helping her slowly move a column of toy animals across the floor, each two inches at a time. The new activity expressed an embodied meaning related to a significant aspect of the trauma she had experienced, namely when being fed. At the start of a session, she began to line up toy animals. After placing the third one in line, she paused. Instead of adding more toy animals to the line, she placed a plastic toy dish before each of the three animals. Then she carefully placed three wooden beads on each dish. I noticed that the beads in each dish were exactly the same (a square, a circle, and a diamond). Vera commented that it was time for the animals to eat. She picked up a bead and held it at the mouth of the first toy animal. While feeding each animal, she jiggled it, yelled, "Don't move!" and slapped it vigorously. During this session, and the next several sessions, Vera added toy animals to the row, and I joined, imitating her body movements and mood. For example, after we carefully placed a dish before each toy animal, and then placed the same beads in each dish, I commented, "Wait, I want to check each plate and make sure each plate has the same food. First I'll check squares." I pointed slowly to each dish, "This one yes. This one yes. Etc." Then I checked circles and the other beads. Also imitating Vera, sometimes I moved a toy animal toward its plate and angrily scolded and slapped. Apparently Vera was now experiencing me as totally committed to her. In one session, she repeated a gesture that she had used when she had invited me to move the next animal in line. After she scolded and slapped a toy animal, she paused, turned to me, and pointed at the next toy animal in the row. I smiled, began to feed that toy animal, jiggled it, and then spanked it. During this and the next several sessions, we continued taking turns, feeding, and spanking each of the toy animals we had lined up in a row.

Having experienced being in the same interactive rhythm with Vera for several sessions, and because we were involved in feeding animals exactly the same amount of food (one aspect of her past traumatic experiences), I decided to initiate a microenactment. My intention with the enactment was to cultivate some reflexivity in her rigid, inner cognitive-emotional orientation and instrumental-expressive behavior, and to stimulate her to perceive and include relevant information from the outer world. Before one session, I placed two sticks of gum in my mouth. After Vera arrived, as we lined up toy animals, dishes, and wooden beads and then fed the animals, I chewed the gum conspicuously. I repeated this for two sessions. At one point Vera asked, "What's in your mouth?" I replied, "Gum." I felt very excited when she responded, "Can I have some?" I gave her a stick of gum. The way she chewed while we fed toy animals suggested that she was imitating me. During the next several sessions, as we continued placing toy animals in a row, and setting dishes with wooden beads before each one, she asked for two sticks of gum. Gradually she increased the number, so that at one point she vigorously chewed five sticks.

In one session after stuffing her mouth with sticks of gum, Vera stopped lining up toy animals and dishes and sat on the floor. I was not clear what she had in mind and sat next to her. She located a dish before each of us and carefully placed wooden beads on each. Then she asked me to feed her. I picked up a bead from her plate, slowly moved it to her mouth, held it near her lips, and she playfully pretended to munch on it. Then she held a bead to my lips and I imitated her. We repeated this play with beads and chewing gum for a few sessions. In one session related to the issue that in the orphanage children were struck with a spoon if they reached up and touched the food when being fed, I decided to enact this. Given the progress Vera had made enacting aspects of the traumatic environments she experienced, I wanted to explore if this body experience would contribute to Vera continuing to develop more reflexivity between her I-Self and Me-Self. When Vera raised a bead to my lips, I touched it with my fingers. Vera yelled, "Don't touch!" and slapped my hand. When I held a bead to her lips, she touched it and insisted I slap her hand, and I did.

Apparently, by repeating this enactment with our bodies during the following weeks, Vera revised the embodied meaning of the trauma she had experienced when being fed at the orphanage. At the start of a session, after I placed a stick of gum in my mouth and offered one to her, she commented, "Can I have some fruit?" I replied. "Sure!" and rushed to the clinic's kitchen, returning with grapes and strawberries. I noticed that Vera had already lined up a row of toy animals. While she nibbled on the fruit, we fed beads to the animals. At the start of each of the next several sessions, Vera asked for fruit, later adding crackers and granola bars, and invited me to join her. Also, given the change that had taken place in the meaning she now was experiencing when eating, in one session I held a grape to her mouth, which she accepted and chewed with pleasure. I was pleased that she did the same with me. During the next few sessions as we fed each other, she asked me about my country of origin and the meals we enjoyed, and also shared meals that were enjoyed in her country of origin. At one point she picked up a couple of beads. Smiling, she handed me one. "Take this and cook something from Sicily, and I'll use this one to cook something from Romania." We played this game for several sessions, ate with pleasure, and continued discussing various meals. Vera's participation in this series of enactments indicated that her rigid inner cognitive-emotional orientation was continuing to develop flexibility so that her I-Self was giving attention to aspects of the outer world related to her embodied meanings.

The next phase of Vera's therapy took place from the second month of her first-grade year until the following spring. During this period of seven months, the reflexivity between her I-Self and Me-Self continued to increase to a significant degree. At the start of one session Vera made a request illustrating that the fantasy mode was now more active, rehearsing issues and meanings related to trauma she had endured. She commented that she would like to make up a story about a person who "wants to run away" and asked me to start the story. During this and the next few sessions I elaborated a story that I hoped would stimulate Vera's fantasy mode to participate in managing the trauma she had endured. The story I invented was about a girl who is trapped in a building with other children, and they all wanted to escape. As I composed the beginning of the story Vera yelled, "They live in an orphanage!" I elaborated the story during the next sessions, noting that one day the girl crawled out of a window and ran into a nearby forest. At this point Vera related the story to her past, shouting, "People in the orphanage are yelling come back!" I continued developing the story. In one session I added that a bird flew by and asked the girl why she was upset. The girl replied she wanted to live in a place without being afraid. The bird led the girl to a safe place. While developing this story, I enacted scenes and sometimes invited Vera to join me. For example, when I shared that the girl crawled out of a window to escape, I crawled back and forth across the playroom floor. While crawling, I asked Vera to join me and she crawled behind me with enthusiasm. As another example, when I shared the conclusion of the story about the bird leading the girl to a safe place, I walked back and forth in the playroom waving my arms, imitating a bird flying. I asked Vera to join me and she participated with vigor, flapping her arms as she walked back and forth behind me.

At the start of the next session, for the first time, Vera did not barricade the door. Related to this significant change in behavior, she made a request indicating that the enactments we had shared during the past months (e.g., chewing gum, play-eating beads and being slapped, eating fruit, playing the girl who wants to escape) had gradually cultivated her I-Self to enter the outer world for her Me-Self to experience. Vera asked if we could go outside. I was surprised and very pleased, because we had not entered the therapeutic garden since the start of her treatment. I responded that it would be great if we explored the outside together. Vera gathered a handful of wooden beads, slowly walked into the garden, and sat under a large bush. I sat alongside of her. For a few minutes she scanned the garden and then exclaimed, "Look, in that bush over there! Those are danger eyes looking at us." She quickly placed the wooden beads on the ground in a row before us. Pointing to the beads she commented, "Now, no one can see us," elaborating that the beads protected us. During the next five weeks, Vera sat under the same bush, imagined danger eyes staring at us, and placed wooden beads around us to ensure our safety. These activities indicated that not only was her I-Self and cognitive-emotional orientation now prepared to engage the outer world, but also that her instrumental-expressive behavior had also become more flexible so that the fantasy mode was continuing to engage in rehearsing and resolving traumatic meanings. Of note, during these weeks, Vera's parents informed me that for the first time she was wetting her bed at night. I shared my opinion with them that this was probably related to the fear and anxiety she was experiencing since she has now entered the outside world physically and psychologically.

During the next month, Vera elaborated working through her experiences with traumatic environments by spending several consecutive sessions either in the playroom or in my office engaged in fantasy play that gradually extended the embodied meaning of a regimented environment into the real world she was now negotiating. Instead of moving animals slowly across the floor, she fantasized a school environment. She lined up chairs in a row and a placed doll in each chair, replicating a classroom. She asked me to pretend I was a student, and she played being the teacher. Speaking with a sharp tone she announced to the students, "I'm teaching you to write letters!" and warned them to hold their hands still and not pick up their pencils until she gave the order. Then she printed several letters on a large easel and ordered the child (doll) sitting in the first chair to copy the first letter on a sheet of paper, the second child to write the next letter, etc. Sometimes she hit the doll because the "child" moved before directions were given. Vera also had dolls eat snacks during recess and repeated the stern behavior she used months before when feeding the line of toy animals.

While spending sessions in my office, Vera's behavior also reflected that she was strengthening her attachment and identification with me. She examined and asked questions about rocks and shells collected in baskets, framed photos on the wall, items on the desk, and books on the shelves. She expressed special interest in the photos. For example, one photo was of a village from which my parents had emigrated. While examining the photo, Vera asked many questions about the village and my relatives. At the same time, she discussed family gatherings of her adoptive family and relatives. Apparently, Vera had worked through, with some degree of success, her experiencing environments as demanding and regimented because at the close of this phase her parents shared that Vera had made steady gains academically and socially, surprising school personnel, given that originally they had wondered if she could manage first grade.

During the next five months Vera completed first grade and began second grade. At the start of one session when Vera entered the playroom, instead of continuing the play that she is the teacher of a classroom with dolls seated on rows of chairs, she asked if we could carry the easel to my office. As I carried the easel upstairs to my office, I wondered if Vera was planning to play school in my office. I set up the easel. When the panels of the easel are spread apart they formed an A-frame structure about five feet tall. Vera asked me to spread a large table cloth over the easel, and she placed two pillows under it. She sat under the easel and asked me to sit with her. During several minutes of silence, I wondered what Vera was now representing, but decided not to say or do anything. Then Vera turned to me and commented, "This is our village. It's safe here." She curled up on the floor, resting her head on a pillow, and I did the same. After several minutes of silence, Vera suddenly thumped her feet on the floor and yelled, "Bad guys are trying to get in our village!" I sprang to my knees, crawled out from under the easel, yelled "I'll stop them," and threw vigorous punches at the imaginary enemy. A minute later I stopped punching and exclaimed, "They're gone. We're safe." Vera asked that we lie down and go back to sleep, which we did. She repeated this enactment several times, and each time I vigorously fought the invaders. During each of the following sessions, she repeated this enactment in my office. A few times after a battle occurred Vera complained, "You're not punching hard enough." I realized that sometimes, after having engaged in five or six battles during a period of about twenty minutes, I became tired and found it difficult to be authentic with my vigor and emotions. I thanked Vera for letting me know, and reassured her that I will keep trying to do my best.

In one session, midway through this phase, Vera introduced an elaboration to this play suggesting that she was continuing to experience the calls for action from environments with more reality-based meanings, and was continuing to resolve the traumatic experiences she had endured. She searched through a magazine, cut out a few photos, and called them "ID cards." She directed that anytime someone approached our village, we must check that person's ID card to determine if he was a "bad guy." Now when Vera thumped her feet while we were lying under the easel, I rushed out and shouted, "Give me your ID card!" I picked up the photo that Vera had already placed on the floor, returned to the easel and handed it to Vera. If she determined the person was a "bad guy," I vigorously threw punches. During each session while we were trying to sleep, our village was approached by imaginary persons about fourteen times, and about half of these persons were bad guys.

Vera introduced a significant modification during the final weeks of this phase. She gradually changed the location of our village from my office to the therapeutic garden. This change in location represented that her core self was continuing to negotiate the calls for action from the real, outer world. First she located our village in the hallway just outside my office, then in the playroom, and then outside in the therapeutic garden. In each location she thumped her feet, announcing that someone was coming, and I jumped out from under the easel, obtained the person's ID card, and Vera determined if the person was bad. When our village was located in the therapeutic garden during the last sessions of this phase, Vera introduced a new activity symbolizing that she had resolved her view that the world was dangerous. After an attack took place, Vera announced it was time to eat and set up plates in a row for children in the village. I located sheets of paper in a row and asked that we imagine a child was sitting before each sheet of paper. Vera asked me to give each child "one spoon of oatmeal." A few times Vera pretended that a child grabbed a plate and asked me to slap the child. When I played my part, Vera surprised me commenting, "They're only kids. Calm down." She also played that the children were worried. Vera stood before each sheet of paper and with a soft tone said, "Don't worry. We are getting out of here."

During the next seven months as Vera completed second grade, she shifted the location of our activities from the therapeutic garden back to my office. Again, the revised meaning of our location was initially enacted in my office and gradually extended to the outer world. At the start of a session Vera asked, "Instead of setting up our things outside, can we do it in your office?" I thought to myself that the weather could not be a factor since it was a sunny day. As we set up the easel in the office, Vera commented, "This is not our village, it's our home and no bad guys are coming." She designated locations in the office and hall way as our "bedroom," "kids bedroom," "living room," "kitchen," and directed that she was the mother and I was the father. Various play themes occurred in these locations for several weeks: for example, we prepared dinner; fed the children; I left for work; if Vera needed to go shopping, I took care of the children; Vera thumped her feet to announce the arrival of visitors for whom we had prepared dinner. A few months later Vera used the same material to locate "our house" in the playroom where we repeated the same enactments. During early spring while she was completing second grade, she used the entire therapeutic garden as "our home," designating one area as our kitchen and other areas as the living room, bedrooms, and so on. In this outer environment, we played various games; for example, Vera would go shopping; when I went to work, I telephoned her from my office.

In one session, Vera engaged in an activity that literally related to her having been adopted. Standing by the pond located in the therapeutic garden and watching frogs hop about, she asked me if she could catch a frog. I rushed off and obtained a net attached to the end of a long stick. She tried a number of times to scoop up a frog and eventually was able to catch one. She placed it in a large plastic container in which she poured water, and with a smile called the frog "Lucky." She talked to the frog in a very friendly way, and then returned it to the pond. During each of the following four sessions, she caught a frog and called the frog "Lucky," elaborating that Lucky is an "orphan who needs a home" and that Vera is the "mother" who "adopts Lucky."

At the close of this phase I scheduled a meeting with Vera's adoptive parents to discuss her progress and my recommendation that we design a plan to terminate treatment. The parents shared that Vera had shown steady improvement and was given the "Flexibility Award" by the school principal, an award given each year to the second-grade student who has shown the most progress socially and academically. They also shared that Vera was now eating food with pleasure, was more engaged when interacting with neighbors and relatives, and told a friend of hers that she was adopted. In the parent's opinion this is the first time Vera had openly acknowledged her adoption. Given Vera's progress at home, at school, and in our sessions, I recommended that I meet with Vera until she completes third grade and, during the coming year, we gradually reduce the frequency of our sessions to once per week, than one session every two weeks, and then one session during each of the last two months. I explained that because of her traumatic experiences during the first years of her life, and given the attachment that Vera and I had developed, a gradual terminating process would likely make a positive contribution to her continuing development. The adoptive parents understood and accepted my recommendation.

During the following sessions, as Vera and I played the "home" game in the therapeutic garden, I introduced termination, emphasizing that she had done really well during second grade, and how proud I was that she had won the Flexibility Award. Also, I reminded her of the time when we huddled afraid under the easel, but now we are happy and enjoy ourselves in the garden we call our "home." I shared that we will meet less often and then stop our meetings when she finishes third grade. Vera listened but did not respond. Vera arrived in the next session carrying a box with about six stones. She showed them to me commenting, "I started a collection just like you have" and added that the rocks came from her yard. Whenever she had been in my office, I noticed that she frequently examined my rock collection with interest. Realizing that rocks could be transitional objects symbolizing our relationship, I commented, "Vera, please add a couple of my rocks to your collection. Then, when you have your rocks in your room, I will be there with you." Vera happily added three of my rocks to her collection. At the start of the next several sessions, Vera arrived with her box and went into the therapeutic garden to look for rocks she could also add to her collection. We searched under bushes, and Vera examined each rock we found, selecting certain ones to add to her collection.

Since we not able to search for rocks during the winter months, Vera started a game in the playroom, reenacting with microactivity the same embodied meanings related to her early traumatic experiences that we had enacted with our bodies. This game also illustrated that her fantasy mode was continuing to develop, rehearsing and working through traumatic experiences. She placed a row of blue beads on the floor and carefully placed a circle of "guard beads" around the blue beads. Vera explained that the blue beads were children who wanted to escape but the other beads were guarding them so they couldn't. I responded that I will figure out different strategies to help them. For example, I took another bead, approached the guards, and engaged them in a conversation to distract them so that the children could escape. She seemed pleased with my perseverance and strategies. Vera also asked that we play board games (e.g., checkers). Much to my surprise, sometimes she interacted in ways that were defiant. After reflecting on her behavior, I decided that she was negotiating self-assertion and testing aggression. Influenced by Louis Sander's infant research (discussed in chapter 1), I responded with playful aggressive comments and gestures, allowing her victories. Vera also initiated discussions about friends at school while eating fruit and granola bars. During the spring, near the end of the school year, she shared her anxiety about attending a sleepover camp for a few weeks during the summer. Her parents had suggested this, and Vera had agreed to go. I suggested that it should help if she took with her the rock collection she and I assembled. Vera responded that it was a great idea and commented, "The rocks will keep me company." During our last meeting, I emphasized that I was proud and happy that together we had gotten a lot done, and that she had "graduated" from our meetings. I smiled commenting that for her diploma I am giving her one of my rocks that I had brought back from Sicily. She responded with excitement and asked if she could select another one from the collection, "Then one is you and one is me." I replied that would be great. Vera held both rocks against her heart and with a big smile said goodbye. During the following years, Vera's adoptive parents occasionally informed me that she was continuing to do well academically and socially, had become very invested in gymnastics and piano lessons, and that when interacting with peers she tended to give help, "behaving like a therapist."

Concluding Comments

In my opinion, this case is an excellent example illustrating how and why enactments, providing body experiences with various environments, can revise a rigid, inner cognitive-emotional orientation and instrumental expressive behavior that had been avoiding persons and environments interpreted by the I-Self as dangerous. Initially this rigid, inner orientation, accompanied by rigid behavior, was vividly displayed during many sessions by Vera barricading the door and ignoring me and the environment, while moving a row of toy animals, each an inch at a time, across the play room floor. By helping her barricade the door, kneeling by her side, helping her slowly move the row of toy animals, and later insuring that each toy animal had exactly the same number and types of beads on the plate before them, Vera's Me-Self increasingly experienced me, and her I-Self interpreted my participation as positive and helpful. In addition, Vera's instrumental-expressive fantasy mode became more active and began rehearsing and resolving aspects of the trauma she had experienced. This inference is supported, for example, by Vera setting up a village in my office and fantasizing that invaders continued to attack. This fantasy provided me the opportunity to battle the imaginary invaders, and demonstrate with vigorous body enactments that I would protect her. That her I-Self interpreted my behavior as providing safety is supported by Vera repeating this expression of danger in a series of locations, the last of which represented the outer world (i.e., first the hallway outside my office, then the playroom, and then the therapeutic garden). These changes in location reflected that her Me-Self was gradually becoming more receptive to experiencing the total outside world that had been avoided for years, and also reflected that her I-Self was interpreting persons and environments as potentially safe. In addition, the series of enactments contributed to Vera's I-Self transforming the interpretation of the outer world from a "village under attack" to "our home," so that her I-Self was also now interpreting the outside world as real. This inference is vividly illustrated by Vera "adopting" a frog during the last months of treatment and calling the frog "Lucky." In addition, my participation in enactments contributed to Vera developing a new self and an attachment and identification with me, reflected by her interest in my country of origin and collection of rocks. In conclusion, Vera initially was very detached, raising the question of autism to school personnel. The therapeutic enactments representing fantasies that took place in various environments (office, playroom, therapeutic garden), resolved the physical and emotional trauma she had endured during the first three years of her life, enabling her to internalize positive experiences with her adoptive parents and school environments. Vera's positive development illustrated what Aron (1998b) proposes, noted in chapter 1. In the absence of traumatic experiences, the dialectical relationship between the I-Self and Me-Self is reflexive, such that the Me-Self continues to experience meanings and emotions related to interactions with environments and, at the same time, the I-Self perceives and interprets these experiences.

CONCLUSION

The cases described in this chapter illustrate that when a patient presents a very rigid inner or outer cognitive-emotional orientation, and a very rigid instrumental-expressive behavior he or she constantly uses when responding to and interacting with environments, the therapist should initiate and participate in enactments with the patient. The cases also illustrate how and why the method of enactments provides the patient with embodied experiences that modify his or her cognitive-emotional and behavioral rigidity and cultivates reflexivity. With this achievement the patient is able to relive embodied meanings related to past traumatic experiences that had been held behind a locked door. In addition the cases illustrate that the technique of repeating enactments promotes the development of reciprocal relationships among embodied meanings and the instrumental-expressive action, fantasy, and language modes and the development of a new self. This development enables the patient to establish a positive and productive relationship with the therapist and with persons in his or her personal world. The recommendation that enactments should be emphasized with particular patients relates to a proposal London (1964) made decades ago that therapy should integrate action and insight. My recommendation also relates, in particular, to the following viewpoints Aron (1998b) discusses in his comprehensive chapter, "The Clinical Body and Reflexive Mind" presented in a volume devoted to relational perspectives of the body.

> The body, bodily sensations, bodily experience, bodily metaphors, and bodily imagery play a central role in the psychoanalytic process . . . the psychoanalytic situation entails two individuals jointly processing, experiencing and reflecting on psychosomatic phenomena (p. 3) . . . it is the failure to process information on a symbolic level which is at the very core of the difficulties that result from trauma . . . [and because] these traumatic experiences cannot be processed the body keeps the score (p. 15) . . . patient and analyst (while not literally touching each other's bodies) come to share a psychoanalytic skin-ego (p. 25). . . . Gradually patient and analyst mutually regulate each other's behaviors . . . such that . . . each reaches into the other's guts . . . the analyst must be attuned to the nonverbal, the affective . . . [and] to his or her bodily responses, so that these may be . . . utilized to construct metaphors and symbol that may be [shared by patient and therapist] (p. 26).

In my opinion these statements, and Aron's entire chapter, are illustrated by the cases I described that are intended to encourage therapists to use enactments when indicated.

NOTE

1. This therapy case is reported in more detail in Santostefano, 2004.

FOUR

A Psychoanalytic-Relational Model of Embodied Techniques to Connect a Patient's I-Self and Me-Self

The Path to the Pathway of Reflexivity

Decades ago as the viewpoint of relational psychoanalysis emerged, W. R. D. Fairbarin (1958) proposed that the goal of relational psychotherapy is to help the patient connect the parts into which his or her self has been split by traumatic events, a proposal elaborated by Aron (1998b) and Stern (2002). To develop therapeutic techniques that address this split, I select particular embodied, cognitive, and behavioral parts of the self (described in chapter 1) that become split and very rigid, instead of dialectically related and flexible, because of traumatic events the person experienced early in life. The research studies presented in chapter 2 illustrate how and why the flexibility and dialectical relationships among these parts of the self contribute to a person responding successfully to the calls for action from environments with which a person is negotiating and the related embodied meanings experienced. Also as noted in chapters 1 and 2, when reflexivity exists between a person's I-Self and Me-Self, the Me-Self perceives and experiences embodied meanings stimulated by the calls for action from environments, and the I-Self prescribes and performs instrumental-expressive behaviors that respond successfully to the calls for action from embodied meanings and from the environment. The therapy cases described in chapter 3 illustrate how traumatic experiences that occurred early in life result in a person's self-developing either a very rigid outer cognitive-emotional orientation so that persons and environments are experienced in terms of one meaning, or a very rigid inner cognitive-emotional orientation so that persons and environments are rejected, each orientation avoiding early traumatic experiences. In addition, these therapy cases illustrate how traumatic experiences also result in a person's self-lacking the ability to be reflexive, so that all calls for action from environments are interpreted with the same meaning to which the I-Self responds with the same instrumental-expressive behavior.

To help a patient connect these parts of his or her self that have been split, and have become very rigid, I propose that a therapist design, initiate, and interact with the patient in enactments. The roots of the model I present are related to viewpoints expressed decades ago. Sandor Ferenczi (1920, 1931) proposed that a therapist use what he called the "action technique," with which the therapist asks a patient to engage in an enactment to relive an experience. For example, Ferenczi encouraged a patient to stroke her face and to sing a song that came to mind. Michael Balint (1932, 1934) emphasized that the therapist create an interpersonal relationship in which the patient could experience the therapist as analogous to an infant's caregiver, construct more flexible patterns of interacting, and experience a "new beginning." Franz Alexander (1950, 1956) described the technique of providing "a corrective emotional experience" that helps the patient develop new ways of interacting. Related to these viewpoints, the model I propose defines a particular sequence of enactments the therapist designs and initiates. In this model, however, the therapist joins the patient participating in the enactment. The foundation of my model also follows the assumptions of relational-developmental theory (Overton, 1998). This theory defines development as interrelations among changes that take place within the embodied meanings a person assigns to his or her interactive experiences and changes that take place in the modalities that perceive and express these meanings (cognitive-emotional orientations and instrumental-expressive behaviors). Aron's (1998b) view of the interrelation between body experiences and the reflexive mind, and his statements noted at the conclusion of chapter 3, also relate to the sequence of enactments I propose. In addition, the following statement by Aron is especially related, "It is . . . by both the patient and analyst engaging in a psychoanalytic form of 'playing' with multiple selves and multiple relational configurations . . . that people develop or strengthen their abilities for mentalization and self-reflexive functioning and transcending limited, constricted . . . versions of themselves" (p. 30).

Before describing the phases of enactments I propose, we should pause to consider the definitions of enactment that have been proposed (e.g., Aron, 1996; Ellman and Moskowitz, 1998; Frank, 1999). In one person psychology, enactment refers to a patient's behaviors inside and outside of therapy that satisfy some positive or negative fantasy or image. In relational psychology enactment refers to the different ways a patient and therapist relate and act on one another verbally and nonverbally (Aron, 1998, p. 198). Theodore Jacobs (1991), who Aron (1996) suggests had the most influence in cultivating acceptance of the concept of enactment within psychoanalysis, defines the term as conscious and unconscious, verbal and nonverbal behaviors of the patient and therapist that express meanings as they interact. My definition of *enactment* is related to these proposals and also to the following. Renik (1998) defines enactments as interactions between patient and therapist that provide the patient with corrective emotional experiences and opportunities to change the meanings of past traumatic experiences the patient internalized. Frank (2002) proposes that when enacting during treatment, a patient could relate to the therapist in ways that are similar to how the patient relates in daily life that cause difficulties. Frank also notes that a patient's enactments may be beneficial depending on how the therapist responds.

In the model of enactments I propose, if a patient is relating and interacting during therapy in ways the patient interacts in daily life, and displays a very rigid cognitive emotional orientation and rigid instrumental-expressive behavior, the therapist designs and initiates enactments consisting of a constellation of actions that provide particular body experiences and embodied meanings and invites-encourages the patient to participate with him or her. The model defines five phases of enactments each addressing a developmental goal. The enactments of each phase are designed to provide experiences that stimulate embodied meanings-emotions for the patient's Me-Self to experience and I-Self to interpret related to the goal of the phase being negotiated. Also, as the enactments are repeated the embodied meaning is internalized. Once this is accomplished, the patient's I-Self perceives and interprets the interactions taking place, and performs a related instrumental-expressive behavior that indicates the goal of the phase has been accomplished. The phases of enactments proposed are analogous to the issues that toddlers and caregivers physically negotiate, noted in chapter 1 (e.g., Sander, 1989; Stern, 1985; Beebe and Lachman. 2014). In addition and related to developmental research, my model includes two types of constellations of actions-emotions that the therapist could use to design an enactment: (1) microbody behaviors patient and therapist share; e.g., gestures, facial expressions, holding one's arm in a particular position, verbal expressions, emotional tones; (2) macrobody behaviors, the therapist's whole body and the patient's whole body participate in the enactment. After describing the goal of each phase of enactments, I illustrate the phase by referring to aspects of the therapy cases described in detail in chapter 3.

CYCLES OF ENACTMENTS TO CONNECT THE PATIENT'S I-SELF AND ME-SELF AND CULTIVATE REFLEXIVITY

Phase I: Patient and Therapist Cultivate a Shared Interactive Language and Reciprocal Relationship

During the first months of treatment, given that the patient's Me-Self and I-Self are not connected , the patient and therapist must cope with the same task that an infant and caregiver face, namely negotiating and sharing an interactive language so that each experiences analogous embodied meanings when sharing the same experience. Accordingly during the first sessions of therapy, the therapist pays close attention to the very rigid inner or outer cognitive-emotional orientation that is dominating the patient's experiences and the rigid emotional tone, meaning and instrumental–expressive behavior the patient constantly expresses while interacting. At the same time, the therapist also pays close attention to the feelings and embodied meanings he or she is experiencing while interacting and dealing with the rigidly repetitive behaviors-emotions of the patient. This requirement relates to Aron (1998b) emphasizing "analysts too must be extremely attentive to their own bodies . . . " (p. 28).

Once the therapist recognizes and manages the embodied meaning-emotion he or she is experiencing, and understands the embodied meaning-emotion the patient is rigidly experiencing, the therapist initiates and performs enactments that represent and express the patient's embodied meaning, and invites the patient to participate. These enactments convey to the patient at the body level, "I hear you, I feel what you feel. I'm joining you." In addition, by participating in this enactment, the patient's Me-Self experiences its meaning-feeling, and the patient's I-Self perceives it, establishing a reciprocal attachment-alliance with the therapist. Related to the therapist being attentive to his or her own body, another issue plays an important role in the process of establishing a shared interactive language and a reciprocal relationship. If the therapist expresses irritation or frustration, for example with an emotional tone, facial expression, or gesture, when relating and responding to the patient's rigid cognitive-emotional orientation and instrumental-expressive behavior, it is important that the therapist acknowledge his/her behavior and apologize with words or actions. If this phase is successively negotiated, the patient participates in the enactment with a positive tone and, at some point, elaborates the enactment by adding a behavioral detail. When this occurs, it indicates that the patient has constructed a shared interactive language and reciprocal relationship with the therapist and is prepared to engage the next phase. We now consider aspects of the therapy cases described in chapter 3 to illustrate this phase.

Case 1

During the first months of therapy Larry brought a sheet of paper to each session on which he had written a list of items, and while on the couch carefully read each item and described related details. The list he brought to each session represented his rigid instrumental-expressive behavior, and his description of each item reflected the rigid outer cognitive-emotional orientation that influenced the interpretations assigned to all persons and environments. Initially, my verbal efforts to help Larry free associate and be more flexible continually failed. Because of my lack of success, I experienced myself becoming frustrated and irritated. In one session I spoke to Larry with a tone that expressed these negative feelings which he observed and pointed out. I apologized and expressed regret. At this point I realized that I needed to use an enactment to cultivate a shared interactive language, so that Larry would experience me as allied with him. In one session I brought a sheet of paper on which I had written a list of items related to our previous session and showed it to Larry. I repeated this in each of the following sessions, and Larry asked if he could take a look at my list, indicating he was experiencing me sharing an interactive language. In order to continue cultivating a shared language, I introduced another microbody enactment and invited Larry to do the same with his list of items. After writing my list of items, I reviewed each and then placed a check mark. I shared this with Larry and asked him to do the same. When he arrived for each of the following sessions, he showed me that he also had made check marks on his list after reviewing each item. His behavior illustrated that we were continuing to develop a shared, interactive language. I introduced another microenactment to add to this progress. I showed Larry that instead of check marks now I wrote numbers at the start of each item, the number one before the most important item, the number two before the second most important, and so on. I asked him to do the same with his list. We continued to show each other our ranked list of items at the start of a number of sessions. Then when Larry arrived for a session, he shared with pride that after recording numbers, he decided to rewrite his items so the number one item was at the top of the list, the number two item next, and so on. He asked me to do the same with my list which I did with a positive tone. This elaboration on Larry's part indicated that he and I had developed a shared interactive language and a reciprocal relationship. Accordingly, I introduced another enactment a few sessions later that addressed the goal of the next phase.

Case 2

During the first weeks of therapy, Alice rigidly focused all of her thoughts and anger on her homeroom teacher, Miss Green. Session after session, she spent most of the time yelling about what this teacher did or how she looked. With much effort, I tried to help her regulate this anger and free associate, but achieved no success. Sometimes I felt frustrated and found it difficult to maintain my focus on Alice. In one session, she complained about the tone of my voice that I realized expressed my frustration and in another session complained that I looked away from her as she screamed about Miss Green. During both incidents I apologized with feeling and explained that I was struggling to find ways that could help her. Given this beginning, I introduced an enactment to develop a shared interactive language. I asked Alice to join me in a game. In this game she describes something about Miss Green, and then we take turns yelling for a minute at what Alice had just described. After each of us yelled, she decided who yelled the best. As we repeated this game I did my best to imitate Alice's gestures and emotional tone. Giving Alice control over the rating system contributed to her experiencing a connection with me. For example, on several occasions after we completed this game she spontaneously said to me, "You're doing a good job." Because this response and her interactions indicated that we had developed a shared interactive language and reciprocal relationship, I introduced a new enactment addressing the goal of the next phase.

Case 3

At the start of our first sessions, although Vera accepted the objects I handed her to barricade the door of the playroom, for several weeks she slowly walked about the playroom as if I and the toys on the shelves did not exist. This behavior vividly reflected her very rigid inner cognitive-emotional orientation. During these sessions, I sat on the floor at one end of the playroom, waiting for Vera to relate to me. Because she did not relate to me with some gesture, in one session I took a toy animal from a shelf, crawled on my knees and slowly walk it on the floor for a minute. After repeating this enactment during several sessions, I noticed that occasionally she would pause for a minute and glance at what I was doing. Perhaps stimulated by this enactment, at one point she placed three toy animals on the floor in a row, and slowly moved each a few inches forward in turn. During the next sessions, she added toy animals to the row, slowly moved them across the floor, and continued ignoring me. For the most part, I sat nearby observing her, and sometimes knelt by her side for a few minutes helping her move the toy animals across the floor. Experiencing this for several weeks, sometimes I became bored and made an interactive error on a couple of occasions, In an effort to help her interact with me and elaborate the meaning of this activity, I picked up one of the toy animals in line, commenting it would like to play. Very irritated, Vera shouted, asking me to be quiet. I apologized and gently stroked the toy animal. In an effort to contribute to our developing a shared interactive language and to repair the mistake I had made, during this and the following sessions, I remained by her side for ten or fifteen minutes, crawled along the floor, and assisted her moving the row of toy animals. When doing this, I tried to imitate Vera's body movements. As we repeated this enactment during the next several months, I noticed that on occasion after moving a toy animal forward, she paused, looked at me and then looked at the toy animal next in line, indicating that it was my turn. In response, I took the toy animal and moved it forward. That Vera was asking me with nonverbal behavior to move a toy animal indicated that we were developing a shared interactive language. Accordingly, during the subsequent months, I remained by her side for the whole session, helping her move a row of toy animals across the floor and remaining alert to when she wanted me to take a turn.

Phase 2: Patient and Therapist Share Enactments-Embodied Meanings Representing the Split and Lack of Reflexivity between the Patient's I-Self and Me-Self

Relying on the shared interactive language and reciprocal relationship developed during the first phase, the therapist initiates microbody and macrobody enactments that provide the patient and therapist the opportunity to share embodied meanings the patient's Me-Self experiences during encounters with all environments, because of the patient's rigid cognitive-emotional orientation and rigid instrumental-expressive behavior. The goal of the enactments of this phase relates to Aron's (1998b) metaphor, noted earlier, that as the patient and therapist regulate each other's behaviors, "each gets under the other's skin" (p. 25–26). From the point of view of this metaphor, the enactments the therapist now initiates are designed to provide body experiences that express to the patient, "I, the therapist, am experiencing your rigidity and lack of reflexivity. Now I feel you under my skin." Related to another metaphor, the goal of this phase provides the patient the opportunity to share with the therapist body experiences representing that the door between the I-Self and Me-Self is closed and locked. If the goal of this phase is achieved, namely that the patient has experienced the therapist under his or her skin, the patient is now prepared and willing to experience being under the therapist's skin which is the goal of the next phase. When the therapist judges that the patient's participation in the enactments has been sufficient, and conveys he or she is united sharing rigidity with the therapist, the therapist initiates an enactment introducing the next phase.

Case 1

Given that Larry and I had developed a shared interactive language (i.e., showing each other our list of items we had reviewed, rewritten, and ranked), I introduced an enactment providing him the opportunity to experience me sharing his I-Self and Me-Self rigidity represented by the list of items he brought and carefully read during every session while on the couch. In one session I placed my sheet of paper and list of items on my head. I explained to Larry that maybe there are other thoughts or memories in my head, so that placing the paper on my head might help them to come out. Then I asked Larry to place his sheet of paper under the pillow on the couch, so that when he is lying down, the list of items he brought would also be near his head and might help other thoughts or memories to come out. After Larry placed his list under the pillow, he asked me whether the list I had placed on my head stimulated other thoughts. To share that I was experiencing the rigidity he experiences, I replied with a tone of frustration that it did not. During the following sessions when we repeated this enactment, I continued sharing that having the list on my head did not stimulate other thoughts, and Larry shared the same. I introduced another enactment to provide him the opportunity to experience with his whole body, and share with me, his cognitive-emotional and behavioral rigidity. Before one session, I arranged the window shades of the six windows in my office so that each was a different distance from the window sill. When Larry arrived, I pointed out to him that all the shades were uneven and asked him to join me in a game for a few minutes before he got on the couch. The game was that each of us would measure the shades of three widows so that the bottom of the shade was exactly four inches from the window sill. I emphasized that by doing this, we would insure that what is inside cannot go out, and what is outside cannot come inside. Also, I noted that after we adjusted our shades, each of us would check the shades of the other. Sometimes I purposely adjusted one of my shades so that it was about a half inch incorrect. Each time Larry discovered my error he cheered and corrected the shade. When he cheered his tone and gestures indicated that he regressed to being a child and was having the opportunity to experience interacting with someone in positive ways, experiences that had not been available in the past. Larry and I repeated this enactment at the start of many sessions. Also, Larry's mood became more positive very likely related to his experiencing me sharing his I-Self and Me-Self rigidity. Because he displayed emotions and behaviors indicating we were united in this rigidity, I introduced an enactment related to the next phase.

Case 2

Given that Alice and I had developed a share interactive language, taking turns yelling about a detail concerning Miss Green that Alice expressed, I asked Alice to draw a picture of Miss Green on a sheet of paper, tapped it on the wall and invited Alice to compete with me yelling at the picture. As we took turns yelling at the picture, I did my best to imitate Alice's tone and gestures. After engaging in this enactment for a series of sessions, Alice asked me to draw a picture of Miss Green that we could yell at which I did with pleasure. In the following sessions we took turns drawing a picture to yell at. Also during these sessions, I purposefully leaned closer toward the picture, an inch at a time, while yelling at it. Alice imitated me so that at one point her nose was an inch away from the picture while she yelled. That Alice had asked me to take turns with her drawing a picture of Miss Green, and that she imitated me leaning closer and closer to the picture while yelling, reflected that Alice recognized that I was experiencing her under my skin, and the lack of flexibility between her I-Self and Me-Self and rigid cognitive-emotional orientation and behavior. Because of this achievement, I introduced a new enactment addressing the goal of the next phase.

Case 3

Given that Vera and I finally developed, to some degree, a shard interactive language and reciprocal relationship, I initiated an enactment related to the split between her I-Self and Me-Self that resulted in her rigid inner orientation and being detached from the outer world. As she repeated slowly moving a row of thirty-four toy animals across the playroom floor, I remained by her side and with a ruler carefully measured the distance she had moved a toy animal to insure it was two inches. Probably influenced by her experiencing me by her side for several months, and helping her carefully move the row of toy animals, she set plates before each of three toy animals and placed the same combination of wooden beads on each plate. To continue sharing that I was experiencing her rigidity, each time she set plates and wooden beads before toy animals, I exaggerated carefully checking the beads on each plate to insure they were exactly the same.

Phase 3: Patient and Therapist Share Enactments-Embodied Meanings that Stimulate Interrelations between the Patient's I-Self and Me-Self and Flexible Cognitive-Emotional Orientation and Instrumental-Expressive Behaviors

The enactments of this phase are very important, especially if the ultimate goal is to help the patient construct insight and re-experience and resolve traumatic meanings-emotions that have been held behind a locked door. At the core of this goal is the concept that if trauma has not been experienced, whenever this person is interacting and communicating with others his or her cognitive-emotional orientation is flexible, traveling on a highway that contains three lanes, namely action, fantasy and language (e.g., Santostefano, 1995, 1998b, 2014, 2015). As noted in chapters 1 and 2, if a patient's I-Self and Me-Self are connected, he/she flexibly shifts from one lane of this highway to another while interacting and sharing thoughts, memories, and feelings with a therapist. Because of this flexibility, this patient and therapist are able to dialectically interact and express meanings-emotions with words, symbols, and actions that eventually result in producing insight and solutions. However, if a patient's I-Self and Me-Self are not connected, the patient maintains a rigid inner or outer cognitive-emotional orientation, and rigidly travels on only one of these lanes, preventing this patient from free associating and relating past experiences held behind a locked door with present experiences. Also, a verbal interpretation is not effective in helping this patient travel on another lane. This viewpoint is vividly illustrated by the case described later, reported by Coppolillo (1987), of a boy who rigidly remained in the action lane playing solitaire card games. When the therapist verbally interpreted to the child the meaning of his playing a solitaire card game, the child responded by vigorously and angrily rejecting the therapist.

Addressing this issue, the enactments a therapist initiates in this phase are designed to provide the patient with body experiences that cultivate cognitive-emotional-behavioral flexibility and the ability to travel on lanes of the highway that have been rigidly avoided. Paralleling how communication takes place during the first years of life between a child and caregiver and how knowledge is constructed (outlined in chapter 1), the interactions a patient and therapist share that are enacted in this phase contribute to the patient developing the ability to flexibly travel on all lanes and cultivate cognitive-emotional interrelations among meanings expressed by action, fantasy, and language. The following, expressed by Piaget (1973) many years ago, based upon his infant research and the viewpoint of cognitive science, in my opinion is related. He noted that becoming conscious of some issue does not involve "shining a light on what is already there [but involves taking] certain unconscious elements and reconstructing them . . . " (p. 257). As noted, the enactments the therapist initiates in this phase provide experiences that reconstruct the interrelations among the patient's action, fantasy and language instrumental-expressive modes and cultivate cognitive-emotional flexibility. Relying on the achievements of the previous phase (i.e., the patient experiencing the therapist getting under and sharing his/her skin) the enactments of this phase provide the patient opportunities to experience getting under and sharing the therapist's skin while traveling side by side with the therapist on one of the lanes of the highway (action, fantasy, or language) that the patient has been avoiding. When the therapist judges this goal has been accomplished, the therapist initiates enactments related to the next phase. The following are examples.

Case 1

In the previous phases, Larry had many opportunities to experience me under his skin because I brought a list of items to each session as he did. Also I placed my list on my head to stimulate other thoughts, and he placed his list under the pillow near his head, but neither of us experienced other thoughts. Also together, we measured window shades so that nothing from the inside can go outside and nothing from the outside can come inside. To address the goal of this phase I introduced several enactments each of which Larry and I repeated during several sessions. First he and I measured window shades so that each was six inches from the window sill, instead of four inches, stressing that now a little from the inside can go out and a little from the outside can go inside. In the following weeks during a series of enactments, we gradually increased and measured the distance of each window shade from the window sill to twelve inches, then twenty-four inches, and then thirty inches. During each of these enactments we emphasized and shared that now a little more from the inside can go outside and a little more from the outside can come inside. These enactments provided Larry with body experiences and embodied meanings that stimulated interrelations among actions (e.g., raising and increasing the height of window shades), fantasies (more from the inside is going outside and more from the outside is coming inside), and language (the meanings we verbalized). That these enactments cultivated I-Self and Me-Self reflexivity and cognitive-emotional-behavioral flexibility is illustrated by Larry free associating, something he had never done to this point. In addition his associations that came to mind indicated that his body was now speaking. For example, he discussed that he has been preoccupied with whether he was sitting "the right way" when at work in his office, because if he wasn't he would not be able to do his "job in the right way." As another example, he shared that before leaving a meeting where he worked that was not over yet, he also wondered if he was sitting in his chair appropriately. The significance of these associations was expressed in the next phase.

Case 2

Given that Alice and I had developed a reciprocal relationship and then shared her rigidity while yelling at pictures of Miss Green that Alice had sketched, I introduced microbody enactments to provide us with experiences using other instrumental-expressive behavioral modes, in addition to yelling. One enactment included the action mode. Alice and I took turns tearing a sheet of paper as vigorously as possible, on which a picture of Miss Green had been sketched. After each enactment, Alice determined with excitement which one of us tore the hardest and recorded the score. With another related enactment that represented controlling anger in the action mode, I asked Alice to compete with me tearing sheets of paper as slowly as possible instead of as hard as possible. She became very involved, timing each of us with a stopwatch and keeping score. To cultivate Alice engaging the instrumental-expressive fantasy mode, in addition to yelling at a picture of Miss Green, we stood by a window, looked out, and yelled at a tree that we fantasized was Miss Green. At the start of a number of sessions, we spent time vigorously tearing and then slowly tearing sheets of paper on which were sketched pictures of Miss Green, and yelling at a tree that we fantasized was Miss Green. During these sessions, Alice decreased the number of times she yelled about Miss Green and began to free associate, sharing for example a trip she and her parents were planning for the weekend. These developments indicated that the relation between her I-Self and Me-Self was developing some reflexivity. Also, for the first time, this reflexivity was also expressed by her body which was beginning to speak. Occasionally while talking with me, she gently rubbed her stomach with the palm of her hand. I imitated her. Three sessions later she flopped on the analytic couch, held a pillow to her stomach, announcing that she has designed a new therapy. The therapist lies on the couch while the patient sits in a chair and discusses issues. In subsequent sessions I participated enacting lying on the couch and holding a pillow to my stomach. That these various enactments cultivated reflexivity in Alice was expressed in the next phase.

Case 3

Because we had successfully shared her inner oriented rigidity for several months, dominated by our moving a row of toy animals across the floor each two inches at a time, I introduced an enactment to cultivate some reflexivity in her orientation and stimulate her to perceive and include information from the outer world. I placed two sticks of gum in my mouth and chewed conspicuously. After repeating this in several sessions, Vera asked me what I was doing. When I explained I was chewing gum, she asked for some gum. I placed gum in her mouth and she imitated me, chewing vigorously. She repeated this for several sessions and occasionally increased the number of sticks she requested, so that at one point she chewed five sticks, as I also chewed a couple. Given that from the start Vera had displayed a very rigid inner cognitive-emotional orientation that avoided the outer world, the enactments of our chewing gum together cultivated the development of some reflexivity and stimulated her to engage in fantasy play. This achievement was reflected by the following. She stopped lining up and slowly moving a row of toy animals across the floor. Instead she placed a plastic plate before each of us, and we played feeding each other. During several sessions after we enacted my placing gum in her mouth, she located a plastic dish before each of us and wooden beads on each dish. I held a bead to her mouth, playing that I was feeding her, and she played feeding me. Then in one session, after I placed a stick of gum in her mouth, she asked for fruit. During each of the next several sessions she asked for fruit, and then asked for crackers in addition to fruit. In one session we fed each other and continued this interactive enactment for several sessions. Of particular relevance to I-Self and Me-Self reflexivity that was developing, while engaged in these enactments, Vera asked me to describe the meals that were preferred and popular in my country of origin, and she described the meals preferred in her country of origin. In addition, Vera's instrumental-expressive fantasy mode continued to be active. For example, we played at cooking meals that are popular in our countries of origin.

Phase 4: Enactments that Stimulate and Express Embodied Meanings Representing Trauma the Patient Experienced and Solutions to the Trauma.

Related to Aron's metaphor (1998b, p. 25), if the previous phases have been adequately negotiated, the patient and therapist now share the same skin and guts, enabling them to experience and share the same embodied meanings. Also, given that the door between the patient's I-Self and Me-Self has been unlocked, the enactments of this phase provide experiences with embodied meanings representing aspects of the trauma the patient had endured and that, to this point, have remained underground. In addition and a core goal of this phase, other related enactments are introduced to elaborate, revise, and eventually resolve these traumatic embodied meanings. The following are examples from the cases described in chapter 3.

Case 1

In the previous phase, the enactments of gradually raising the window shades from four inches from the window sill to thirty inches, so that more from the inside can go out and more from the outside can come in, resulted for example in Larry free associating as to whether he was sitting in the "right way." Because of this achievement, I introduced an enactment that provided an embodied meaning symbolizing that all of what is inside is free to go outside and all of what is outside is free to go inside. I pulled down a window shade a few inches from the window sill and released it so that it quickly rolled up to the top of the window. I called this the "Fly Free" game and asked Larry to participate. Initially he was tense when releasing a window shade, but eventually expressed very positive, playful emotions as he repeated this enactment. After repeating this game for about ten minutes at the start of the next several sessions, I introduced another enactment to contribute to Larry further cultivating I-Self and Me-Self reflexivity so that unconscious, embodied meanings could be experienced and expressed. After releasing a window shade, Larry and I took turns pouring water out of a bottle into a pan so that the water could "flow free." He became very involved when participating and indicated that his body had integrated the meanings of the two enactments. For example after pouring water out of the bottle, he exclaimed, "It's really free to flow down the river. Now whatever is inside can go out."

After repeating these two enactments for three sessions, for the first time Larry arrived without a list and discussed with much anxiety a nightmare he had experienced the previous night in which he is falling down a huge pipe through "black space." That the door between Larry's I-Self and Me-Self was now totally open, and that he had developed reflexivity, was vividly demonstrated by his associating to this nightmare. He recalled with much emotion the trauma he had endured as a child when his mother required him to call her after he had a bowl movement so she could count the stools. She slapped him whenever he flushed the toilet and left the bathroom without calling her. Larry continued working hard to resolve these traumatic experiences.

Case 2

The various enactments Alice and I had engaged during the previous phases opened the door between her I-Self and Me-Self and promoted reflexivity. This achievement is vividly illustrated by the traumatic memories she experienced while lying down in a prone position on a mount. Lying on the mount reminded her of lying on her mother's belly when mother was pregnant. From this embodied memory, she eventually addressed and resolved traumatic experiences related to the death of her newborn sister and to her mother's absence for a number of months, and depression for years. In addition Alice introduced an enactment that also vividly illustrated the reflexivity that had developed. Instead of throwing rocks at a tree that we had called Miss Green (her homeroom teacher), she now called the tree "Mother" and another tree, "Sister." She initiated that we throw rocks at each tree and exclaim something about the pain they had caused. Repeating these enactments indicated that Alice's instrumental-expressive behaviors had also developed flexibility. During her grade-school years she had constantly yelled about teachers, and recently in high school about her homeroom teacher. Now the action mode (throwing rocks) was interacting with the fantasy mode (imagining the tree to be Miss Green, and later imagining two trees to be Mother and Sister). The flexibility of her behavioral modes, as well as the I-Self and Me-Self reflexivity, cultivated by enactments, now enabled her to re-experience and resolve her trauma.

Case 3

A particular behavior on Vera's part that occurred in this phase of her therapy is especially significant. She did not barricade the door, and I did not search for items for her to use. This indicated that her very rigid inner cognitive-emotional orientation had become a little more flexible and her core self was now able to engage the outer world, which had been avoided for years. In addition, not barricading the door also indicated that her inner self was prepared to experience and express traumatic embodied meanings that had been held behind a closed door. For example, when eating fruit, Vera reenacted what she had experienced at the orphanage. She slapped my hand when I touched the fruit she was holding to my lips, and asked me to slap her hand when she touched the fruit I held to her lips. Vera extended this issue into another aspect of the outer world she was now experiencing. Fantasizing a classroom, she lined up chairs, seated a toy animal on each, and played being a teacher and ordered the children not to touch their pencils until she gave permission or else they would be slapped.

During another series of sessions, Vera also re-experienced aspects of trauma that occurred at the orphanage. She asked that we locate an easel in my office on the second floor and lie under it. While we pretended we were sleeping, she thumped her feet, indicating that "bad" persons were approaching. In response, enacting that I would protect us, I jumped up, threw vigorous punches at the imaginary enemy, and announced we were safe. She repeated this theme in the play room on the first floor, and then in the therapeutic garden. This sequence of locations indicated that her I-self and Me-self were engaging the outer would as well as re-experiencing trauma. Related to this issue, two other themes were enacted during other sessions. With one theme she asked me to make up a story about a girl who "wants to run away" and be safe. I developed a story about a girl who crawls out of a window into the outside world. A bird flies by, offers help and guides her to a safe place. I enacted the story as I shared it, and invited Vera to join me which she did. For example, we crawled on the playroom floor pretending we were crawling through a window to escape, and we ran about waving our arms, pretending we were the bird that offered to guide the girl to a safe place. In terms of the second theme, Vera asked to go outside into the therapeutic garden. She sat under a bush and I sat by her side. She fantasized that "danger eyes" in a nearby bush were watching us. We located wooden beads before us that prevented the "danger eyes" from seeing us. The reflexivity Vera developed, in addition to flexibility in her cognitive-emotional orientation and instrumental expressive behaviors, enabled her to experience embodied meanings representing the trauma she had endured and negotiate solutions. Given this achievement, as noted in the next phase, she engaged the outer world and no longer presented herself as if she was autistic.

Phase 5: Enactments that Provide the Patient's New Self with Experiences and Encourage the New Self to Engage the Outer World

At this point the patient has relived and resolved the embodied meanings that represent past traumatic experiences. This achievement has enabled the patient to develop a new self that now includes reflexivity between the I-Self and Me-Self and flexibility in his or her cognitive-emotional orientation and instrumental-expressive behavior. Accordingly, the focus of this phase is to introduce enactments that provide the patient's new self with embodied experiences that symbolize and cultivate confidence interacting and negotiating with the outer world. In addition, whenever indicated, the enactments are designed to provide the patient experiences that engage aspects of the outer world the patient's previous pathological self has avoided. The following are examples.

Case 1

Larry developed a new self as he free associated to his nightmare and resolved the traumatic embodied meanings related to his mother requiring him to remain on the toilet until she checked his bowl movement, and spanked him if he did not. I introduced an enactment that would stimulate this new self to engage the outer world. In general, the enactment related to two issues. He had made it clear that his father rarely was interactive and playful, so that Larry found it difficult to be playful with his children. The other issue was that he had expressed gratitude when I held his hand while he described with much anxiety his nightmare about falling through black space down a huge pipe. I invited him to step outside with me, since he and I had accomplished that whatever is outside is free to go inside and whatever is inside is free to go outside, a metaphor we had shared many times while engaging the window shade enactments. He responded with pleasure and, as we walked about, he touched bushes and expressed that now he feels his "arms are around the outside world." At one point he noticed horseshoes, and I invited him to play for a few minutes which he did with pleasure. Then he asked if we could play horseshoes at the start of each of the next sessions, "like we used to play the window shade games." At the start of the next several sessions we played horseshoes for about ten minutes, and Larry experienced and expressed much pleasure and excitement when competing with me. Also during these sessions, Larry shared that his wife has been very pleased because he is now spontaneous and reciprocal with her, for example helping empty the dishwasher and folding laundry. In addition he shared that he has been playing games with his children and emphasized that he is teaching his son to play horseshoes so that he can become as good as I was, reflecting Larry's positive identification with me. Larry's new self was also experienced in his work environment. For example, the young man whom he supervises, and who in the past had experienced Larry has detached and critical, told him "now I feel we're a team."

Case 2

The new self that Alice developed was exhibited in several ways. For several sessions she and I walked about the therapeutic garden where she had previously experienced embodied meanings related to the trauma she eventually resolved. Now as we engaged the outdoors, the embodied meanings she experienced were positive. She named a tall evergreen tree "'Mom,' because it is really nice." Since there was no small evergreen tree she could name in honor of her deceased sister, I obtained one. Alice planted it with much positive emotion, and noted that in the coming years she will ask her parents to visit the garden with her, once in a while, so that she can watch her sister growing up. Alice added that when she comes by to see her sister, it would also give her a chance to spend a few minutes visiting with me. This illustrated that Alice's instrumental-expressive behaviors had become flexible and the fantasy mode (a tree representing deceased sister) was now assisting her managing the loss of a sister. Alice's request to visit me for a few minutes in the future also illustrated that she had developed a positive identification with me. Also, in the last phase of our sessions, I introduced an enactment, inviting her new self to take turns with me and slowly chew a cracker. Related to these enactments, her parents reported that Alice no longer went to her room to binge eat. Now she had dinner with them, and they were pleased that she seemed relaxed, spontaneously sharing experiences at school and with friends. Also related to her new self, the school counselor reported that Alice no longer expresses anger at her homeroom teacher and has cultivated friendships with classmates. Alice's positive identification with me is also illustrated by her asking for a stone from my collection during our last session which she held with much feeling.

Case 3

In sharp contrast to the rigid inner cognitive-emotional orientation and rigid instrumental expressive behavior that had resulted in Vera isolating herself from the outer world and behaving as if she was autistic, her new self now engaged and interacted with the entire therapeutic garden to represent our "home" where she and I played being parents. For example, she designated one area of the garden our kitchen, and other areas our living room, the children's bedroom, our bedroom, and so on. That she developed flexibility in her instrumental expressive behaviors is also illustrated by her fantasy mode now rehearsing and resolving traumatic meanings we had negotiated with our total bodies and actions. She placed a line of wooden beads on the floor of the playroom, fantasized them as "children who want to escape," and surrounded these with other wooden beads she fantasized as "guards." I participated in this fantasy play, distracting the guards so that the children could escape. Also, when she engaged the therapeutic garden, I helped her catch a frog in the pond. She fantasized adopting it and called it "Lucky." That Vera's new self had developed a positive identification with me is illustrated by the following. She became interested in the collection of rocks that I had in my office. She arrived for one session with a collection of rocks, noting that she was imitating me. For several sessions we enacted searching for rocks throughout the therapeutic garden to add to her collection. During our last session, I gave her one of my rocks to add to her collection. She asked for another and I invited her to take one. When she selected one she commented, "This way one is you and this one is me." That Vera's new self was engaging the outer world is also dramatically displayed by the following. At the close of second grade, she was given the "Flexibility Award" by the school principle, an award given each year to a second-grade student who had shown the most progress academically and socially. Vera displayed this progress during third grade. Also, the parents shared that she was now interacting with neighbors and, for the first time, had discussed with a friend that she had been adopted. In addition they shared was helping friends, "acting like a therapist."

WHAT IS REQUIRED OF A THERAPIST TO CONDUCT THESE PHASES OF ENACTMENTS?

The Therapist Should Abandon Emphasizing Words and Interpretations When Indicated

When working with an adult or child who lacks reflexivity, displaying a rigid cognitive-emotional orientation and a rigid instrumental-expressive behavior, the first requirement that a therapist must consider and manage is to abandon emphasizing the use of words in order to help the patient discuss and elaborate issues, meanings and emotions that are causing him or her difficulties. This requirement relates to Greenberg's (1996) historical review of the tension that developed between psychoanalysts who advocated using words and those who advocated using acts "that led many classically trained analysts to dismiss what . . . interpersonalists were doing as 'mere' psychotherapy" (p. 201). Along the same line, in an article addressing the need to train analysts to work with embodied expressions, Sletvold (2012) notes, "Analytic training, as well as psychotherapy training generally, has tended to privilege the exchange of words" (p. 410).

Coppollillo (1987) describes an episode that took place during psychotherapy, vividly illustrating a therapist facing the requirement of abandoning the use of words. The episode concerned a boy who for many sessions presented himself as "guarded, reluctant to reveal anything about himself and showed little inclination to explore the significance of anything" (p. 215). In one session this boy again began to play a game of solitaire with a deck of cards he had brought with him. (From the viewpoint of the model presented in this text, this boy was displaying a rigid inner cognitive-emotional orientation and a rigid instrumental-expressive behavior.) In this session, the therapist decided to interpret the boy's behavior. "'Do you suppose by playing solitaire, you're showing me how it feels to be ignored?' The boy responded, 'No solitaire. Just sit here and talk to this old shit-head, son-of-a-bitch.' With this the boy walked away and handled some items in a disinterested way" (p. 215). The boy's response makes clear that the therapist's verbal interpretation failed. How the therapist could have responded following the model I propose is illustrated below.

The Therapist must be Familiar With and Use His/Her Embodied Meanings

The requirement of recognizing when to abandon the use of words (illustrated by Coppolillo's episode) relates to another requirement a therapist faces in order to implement the technique of enactments. A therapist must be familiar with the embodied meanings-emotions he or she experiences when interacting with a patient and also recognize whether his or her embodied meanings-emotions are interfering with the therapeutic relationship and with using enactments versus words. Sletvold's (2014) outstanding volume, *The Embodied Analyst* is especially related to this requirement. He provides a comprehensive review of the nonverbal and affective aspects of the analytic process that contributes to an integration of nonverbal and embodied experiences in relational psychoanalytic theory. He also describes techniques supervisors could use to help candidates work with embodied expressions to make unconscious relational experiences conscious. In addition, he emphasizes the importance of therapists understanding how their embodied meanings influence them when working with patients. Along the same line, a volume edited by Anderson (2008) includes several papers that describe various "body techniques." A therapist might dismiss enactments as "mere" psychotherapy because the use of enactments requires this therapist to be aware of his or her embodied meanings, body language and interactive style, a requirement that is very demanding.

Returning to Coppolillo's example as an illustration, how could the therapist have responded to satisfy the requirement of recognizing one's embodied meanings in order to abandon words and use enactments? If this therapist acknowledged to himself that he felt insulted and irritated because the boy was again ignoring him, and accepted other ways of responding to this boy, he could have followed the first phase of enactments, discussed above, which addresses the task of developing a shared interactive language with the patient. When the boy again occupied himself playing a game of solitaire, the therapist could have taken a deck of cards, sat at the far end of the room, and occupied himself playing a game of solitaire with a friendly attitude and behavioral style, so the child would not have experienced that he is being mocked. By repeating this enactment, the therapist would express to the patient, "I hear what you're saying. I know what it feels like to want to be away from others." Instead of using such an enactment, this therapist made an interpretation that could have been influenced by the therapist feeling ignored, insulted and irritated. The embodied meanings-emotions this therapist very likely experienced takes us to a requirement that all therapist should manage.

As discussed in chapter 1, the experiences a person has with his/her body forms the foundation of the Self (e.g., Aron and Anderson, 1998; Beebe and Lachman, 2014; Sander, 1989; Stern, 1985; Piaget, 1951). This concept not only applies to patients but also to therapists. Accordingly, and especially when working with a patient who lacks reflexivity, and rigidly repeats meanings-emotions and behavior, a therapist is required to be familiar with the embodied meanings-emotions he/she experiences when interacting with this patient and acknowledge if he or she feels, for example, uncomfortable, tired, bored, or irritated. Whenever these embodied meanings-emotions occur, it is important that the therapist recognize how the feelings influence the way he/she is interacting and apologize to the patient in the service of continuing to develop a shared interactive language. This issue relates to counter-transference.

In the preface I describe my early experiences that emphasized the importance of embodied meanings-emotions, forming a major part of my self. This aspect of my self was expressed, for example, during graduate school when I designed the Miniature Situation Test and during academic positions where I continued to conduct research that explored meanings-emotions expressed by the body. Influenced by this personal history, sometimes my self felt bored or irritated, if a patient rigidly and repeatedly verbalized some issue or repeated a behavior, resulting in my making interactive errors. I provide examples in each of the cases described in chapter 3. For example, when Larry carefully read a list of items he had prepared during each of our first sessions, I felt bored and irritated. In one session this embodied meaning-emotion influenced how I expressed myself, a tone that Larry noticed. I apologized verbally and also by introducing the first enactment. I brought a list of items to the next session that I shared with Larry. This contributed to our cultivating the beginning of a shared interactive language, and Larry experiencing me as joining him. Similarly, I become bored when Alice continued yelling about her homeroom teacher, and expressed this embodied meaning-emotion by occasionally looking away from her and glancing at a nearby shelf of books. Alice noticed this and angrily complained. I apologized verbally and also by introducing our first microbody enactment. I asked Alice to describe some detail about her home room teacher. Then I joined her yelling about the detail, and she decided who yelled the best. This initial enactment helped Alice experience me as joining her and launched the shared interactive language we developed. With regard to Vera, initially she walked slowly about the playroom and ignored me, an interpersonal situation similar to the episode Coppolillo described, noted earlier. Then during several sessions she devoted the total hour slowly moving a row of toy animals across the floor one inch at a time. I became bored and thought I could cultivate more meaning to this ritual by picking up one of the toy animals and pretended it wanted to play. Shouting with irritation, Vera made clear that I made a mistake. I apologized verbally but also by introducing the first enactment. I remained kneeling by her side for many sessions, occasionally moving one of the toy animals an inch forward, and did not say or do anything else. This enactment contributed to Vera experiencing me as joining her and participating in a shared interactive language.

In conclusion, when a therapist's embodied meanings influence the therapist to make an interactive error, the therapist apologizes not only verbally but by enacting the patient's verbal and nonverbal behavior. Also, it takes time and effort for a therapist to become aware of his/her embodied meanings and body language (e.g., Pruzinsky, 1990; Cash and Pruzinsky, 2002; Sletvold, 2014). In addition to a therapist cultivating awareness of his/her embodied meanings and body language, a therapist must also notice whether the rhythm and tone of embodied meanings he/she is using are similar to the patient's. The importance of this issue relates to interpretation, that is whether the patient understands the message being communicated. I have proposed (Santostefano, 2004) that the embodied meanings of the therapist and those of the patient are engaged in continuous dialectal interactions that express meanings. This issue as Aron (1996) elaborates is illustrated by the following. He notes, "Interaction is in itself interpretive, which is to say conveys meaning . . . (p. 214) . . . interpretation is an interpersonal participation. It is an observation from within the interaction rather than from outside of it" (p. 118) . . . meaning is negotiated and co-constructed. Meaning is arrived at through a meeting of the minds—a patient's and therapist's" (p. xii).

The Therapist Must Repeat Enactments Many Times with the Patient in Order to Negotiate the Goal of Each Phase and for the Patient to Develop a New Self

Because the model I propose requires a therapist to communicate with body language when interacting with an adult or child patient, this requirement may run into the same obstacles that are faced by a caregiver who is attempting to grow together with an infant. Similar to an infant and caregiver interacting during the first months and years of life, a patient who lacks I-Self and Me-Self reflexivity and the therapist are foreign to each other during the first months of therapy. In infant development, in order to negotiate developmental issues that eventually result in a sense of self, the infant requires the opportunity to engage repeatedly in interactions with the caregiver for many months, and the caregiver is required to participate and negotiate during these interactions. This viewpoint is illustrated by the comprehensive research reported by Beebe and Lachman (2014) who address origins of attachment and its importance for adult therapy. They studied face to face interactions that took place between infants and caregivers for many months and note, for example, "it is now increasingly understood that the bodily or implicit aspects of communication is not only necessary . . . but an essential component of the very capacity to communicate . . . " (p. xix). The requirement that a patient who lacks reflexivity must have repeated bodily experiences with a therapist, as does an infant with a caregiver, in order to develop a new self is also illustrated by the research programs of Stern (e.g., 1985) and Sander (e.g., 1989) noted in chapter 2. Stern focuses on how interactions that are repeated between infant and caregiver result in the infant developing a sequence of "senses of self." Sander focuses on how, during the first three years of life, an infant and caregiver use body language when interacting in order to "negotiate" a series of developmental issues, negotiations that contribute to the infant eventually developing a self. Stern's and Sander's research projects, as well as the research by Beebe and Lachman (2014), emphasize that repeating two or three interactive experiences does not accomplish the task of an infant-toddler developing a sense of self. Rather, interactions that are repeated eventually provide embodied experiences symbolizing the issue being negotiated. Related to these research projects, if a patient lacks reflexivity, and is handicapped by a rigid cognitive-emotional orientation and rigid instrumental expressive behavior, he or she must have the opportunity to interact and negotiate repeatedly during enactments with the therapist, in order for the patient to develop a new self and a positive identification with the therapist. This new self should include cognitive-emotional flexibility and dialectical relationships among the instrumental-expressive modalities of action, fantasy and verbal behaviors, each serving the patient as he or she negotiates and interacts with others and environments.

Conclusion

In one of his publications that had a significant influence on the rise of relational psychoanalysis Aron (1996) asks, "How much does the analyst get caught up with the patient in therapeutic action? How much is the analyst involved in enactments and interaction" (p. xii)? My response to both questions is, "one hundred percent" when an adult and child patient is handicapped by a rigid cognitive-emotional orientation, rigid instrumental-expressive behavior and lacks I-Self and Me-Self reflexivity. As noted, these cognitive and behavioral disabilities resulted from early traumatic experiences and focus on what is not relevant to help the body and mind avoid recalling and re-experiencing the trauma. Accordingly, in order to develop cognitive-emotional-behavioral flexibility and a new self, these patients must "have a new experience rooted in a new relationship" (Aron, 1996, p. 214). The relational psychoanalytic concept of providing a patient with new experiences rooted in a new relationship has stimulated much interest in the issue of enactment, resulting in various definitions. Accordingly, I pause to underscore the definition of enactment I propose by relating it to Grossmark's definition (2012). He provides a very useful historical review of the shift that has occurred in psychoanalysis from an emphasis on free association to an emphasis on "flow of enactment engagement" (p 287). He notes, for example, "The analyst accompanies, even shares in the journey that both participants take as the field unfolds and tells its story . . . a story is told in the events, interactions, affects and states that emerge in the analytic couple" (p. 289). Grossmark illustrates these issues by describing his emotional and vigorous participation during psychotherapy he conducted with a young man. The flow of enactments that took place were verbal and emotionally intense exchanges. This flow of interactions enabled this man to overcome the trauma he had experienced when a child.

In contrast, the therapeutic model of enactments I propose defines enactments as macrobody and microbody physical actions, sometimes accompanied by words, that the therapist designs, initiates and participates in, providing patient and therapist the opportunity to share experiences that stimulate particular embodied meanings. In addition, the phases of enactments the therapist prescribes are related to and replicate aspects of the process of "growing together" that takes place between an infant-toddler and caregiver, resulting in the patient developing a new self. My model also proposes that an important part of a person's self is flexibility in the process of cognitive-emotional orientation and in the process of instrumental-expressive behavior as the person responds to embodied meanings stimulated by the environment with which the person is negotiating. The significance of this matrix of cognitive, emotional, behavioral, and environmental processes is illustrated by the studies described in chapter 2. In addition, my model proposes that these processes play an important role in a person's I-Self and Me-Self reflexivity, providing a person the capacity to interact and negotiate successfully with human and nonhuman environments and benefiting from interrelating the past with the present.

Related to the comprehensive research of development during infancy cited in chapter 1, Aron (1998b) notes, "In infancy our bodily sensations are greatly affected by the qualities of the 'holding' and 'handling' that we receive from caregivers . . . [therefore] . . . our self is first and foremost a body-as-experienced-being-handled-and-held by the other self, in other words, our self is first and foremost a body-in-relation self" (p. 20). This viewpoint is illustrated by the therapy case studies presented in chapter 3. For these patients because the roots of their pathology lay in early relationships and experiences (the way they were handled), a phase of experiencing had to precede a phase of understanding in order for a cure to occur. For these patients the meanings that had been produced by physically related trauma were not suddenly "understood," as with insight. Rather, repeated body experiences while interacting with, and "being handled" by, the therapist were necessary in order to cultivate flexibility in their rigid cognitive-emotional-behavioral processes. Once this was achieved they were able to construct trauma-related meanings and develop understanding. In addition, for these patients, the body experiences that occurred during physical interactions with the therapist eventually contributed to their developing a new self. As Summers (2001) notes, a relationship negotiated during treatment that does not produce new ways of being and relating "is a rearrangement of old furniture" (p. 639). The phases of enactments I propose are intended to construct new furniture in a person's self. I acknowledge that the phases of enactments are very demanding for a therapist and require considerable practice. Analogous to the task caregivers face during the first years of a child's life, the therapist is required to become "involved" physically and emotionally to serve the patient's developmental needs. This requirement includes enacting a wide range of physical actions, tempos, and emotional tones, while remaining alert to whether the level of involvement is too little or too much in terms of the patient's unique needs.

Interest in body-oriented psychotherapy is growing illustrated, for example, by Young's (2010) review of the development of Body-Psychotherapy in Europe and by the European Association for Body Psychotherapy (Gill, 2010). In addition Rabinor and Bilich (2011) describe various forms of experiential therapy designed to facilitate change and growth in a patient's body image. Related to the viewpoint of relational psychoanalysis, and to the cognitive-emotional-behavioral model I outline in chapter 1, they note "Because the formation of body image begins at a preverbal developmental stage, techniques designed to encourage nonverbal exploration and expression will be effective at creating change at that level. This level of intervention may be particularly important for clients whose body image disturbances stem from early childhood experiences" (p. 424). In one approach to body-oriented psychotherapy addressing the issue of body image, and related to the Two Person Drawing Test described in chapter 2, Weinberg (2010) describes the use of artistic techniques in group therapy. Each participant was asked to draw a picture of himself/herself and participate in a discussion about the picture with the group members. As another example of the growing interest in body-oriented psychotherapy, in her chapter that addresses the importance of body-mind treatment, Ressler (2009) notes, "The body and mind cannot be treated separately . . . the reciprocal relationship between body and mind, language and emotion, client and healer create a pathway to body ownership. . . . Reclaiming the forsaken body means a return to real feelings which can be identified, experienced and expressed" (p. 145). Other investigators have included animals and the outdoors to provide body-oriented psychotherapy. Johansen and colleagues (2014) describe a psychotherapy approach for adolescents and adults, "who have participated in conventional psychotherapy in the past without positive treatment and outcome" (p. 324) and for whom "conversation based psychotherapy was not acceptable" (p. 327). The therapy they propose "involves a triangular relationship between a horse, patient and therapist" (p. 325). The therapist guides the patient to groom, handle, and ride a horse, to provide the patient with "physical, kinesthetic and visual experiences" (p. 327) and to cultivate attachment and nonverbal communication. They also note, "Researchers are increasingly considering the importance of nonverbal communication in psychotherapy. How something is expressed carries more significance and weight than what is actually said." (p. 329).

Within the growing interest in body-oriented psychotherapy, several studies have been reported that bear some relationship to the cognitive-emotional-behavioral model I present in chapter 1 and the research described in chapter 2. (A) Studies related to patients with a rigid, inner cognitive-emotional orientation: Eke and Gent (2010) explored the use of dance-movement psychotherapy in a school setting with a group of adolescents who were withdrawn and found it difficult to verbalize thoughts and feelings. Payne (2009) used dance-movement psychotherapy with a group of patients who presented difficulties they could not explain. Pearson and Wilson (2009) discuss the use of expressive techniques (e.g., body exercise, expressive writing, responding to music) to enhance the participation of a patient in the therapeutic process. (B) A study related to patients with a rigid outer cognitive-emotional orientation: Pylvanainen (2010) used dance-movement therapy with a group to foster each patient's paying attention to his/her body and body sensations. (C) A study related to patients with a rigid instrumental-expressive behavior. Meehums and colleagues (2012) used dance-movement therapy with a group of obese women who were binge eating and presented emotional eating problems.

Interest in body-oriented psychotherapy has also simulated interest in the importance the therapist's body. Related to Sletvold's (2014) volume noted earlier that comprehensively address the embodied analyst, Colosimo and Pos (2015) discuss a model to cultivate a therapist using nonverbal markers to express being present. Along the same line, Blum (2015) discusses the technique of "embodied mirroring, a nonverbal, experiential, relational, body based technique which promotes the client's movement toward health" (p. 115). For example, when a patient expresses he/she is confused and does not know what to say, the therapist explains to the patient, "Through my body, I would like to try to feel and sense what it is like to be you when you are in this state" (p. 119). The therapist then asks the patient to guide the therapist in assuming, for example, body postures and movements that mirror the patient's body experiences. Blum notes, "Mirroring promotes a knowing that the other is with me" (p. 117). The viewpoint of relational psychoanalysis, and growing interest in body-oriented psychotherapy, brings up issues related to the increase in psychotherapy that is being conducted with Skype and the telephone. This issue raises the question whether physical proximity between a patient and therapist is essential in the relational psychoanalytic process, comprehensively discussed by Bayles (2012). In my opinion, if a patient lacks I-Self and Me-Self reflexivity, and is handicapped by a rigid inner or outer cognitive-emotional orientation and by a rigid instrumental-expressive behavior, the physical presence of the therapist and patient is essential so that each can get under each other's skin (Aron, 1998b). This relates to the last issue I would like to address.

Newnham and Page (2010) report that 30 to 35 percent of patients who were offered psychotherapy did not benefit. Along the same line, to explore premature discontinuation in adult psychotherapy, Swift and Greenberg (2012) reviewed 669 studies representing 83,834 clients and report that one in five clients dropped out of therapy prematurely, and reported that the dropout rate was not moderated by the orientation of the therapy. They also note that special efforts should be made to decrease the number of patients who drop out of psychotherapy before treatment is completed. Two of the patients I present in chapter 3 (Larry and Alice) had participated in psychotherapy before I engaged them. From the viewpoint of my model, the majority of the patients that Swift and Greenberg reviewed may have been handicapped by a rigid inner or out cognitive-emotional orientation, a rigid instrumental-expressive behavior and lacked I-Self and Me-Self reflexivity that prevented them benefitting from a traditional form of psychotherapy, especially if it emphasized verbal discourse. I hope the model I present in this volume provides psychotherapists with another lens through which they could examine a patient during their first sessions. This lens should help the therapist determine if the patient is handicapped by cognitive-emotional-behavioral rigidity, lacks reflexivity, and determine if the phases of enactments I propose are indicated. I also hope the model contributes to a "psychotherapy for the people" presented by Aron and Starr (2014) who emphasize that relational psychoanalysis does not have boundaries.

References

Alexander, F. (1950). Analysis of the therapeutic factors in psychoanalytic treatment. *Psychoanalytic Quarterly*, 19, 448–500.

———. (1956). *Psychoanalysis and Psychotherapy: Developments in Theory, Technique and Training*. New York: Norton.

Allport, G. W. and Vernon, P. E. (1933). *Studies in Expressive Movement*. New York: Macmillan.

Amone-P'OlaK, K., Garnefski, N. & Kraai, V. (2007). Adolescents caught between fires: cognitive emotion regulation in response to war experiences in northern Uganda. *Journal of Adolescence*, 30, 655–669.

Anderson, F. S. (Ed.) (2008) Bodies in Treatment: The Unspoken Dimension. New York: The Analytic Press.

Anderson, J. W. (2014). How D. W. Winnicott conducted psychoanalysis. *Psychoanalytic Psychology*, 31, 375–395.

Aragno, A. and Schlachet, P. J. (1996). Accessibility of early experience through the language of origin: A theoretical integration. *Psychoanalytic Psychology*, 13, 23–24.

Aron, L. (1996). *A Meeting of the Minds: Mutuality in Psychoanalysis*. Hillsdale, NJ: The Analytic Press.

———. (1998a). Introduction: the body in drive and relational models. In L. Aron and F. Anderson (Eds.) *Relational Perspectives on the Body*. (pp. xxvii–xix). Hillsdale, NJ: The Analytic Press.

———. (1998b). The clinical body and the reflexive mind. In L. Aron and F. S., Anderson (Eds.) *Relational Perspectives on the Body*. (pp. 3–38). Hillsdale, NJ: The Analytic Press.

———. (2005). On the unique contribution of the interpersonal approach to interaction: A discussion of Stephen A. Mitchell's "Ideas of Interaction in Psychoanalysis." *Contemporary Psychoanalysis*, 41, 21–34.

Aron, L. and Anderson, F. S. (Eds.) (1998) *Relational Perspectives on the Body*. Hillsdale, NJ: The Analytic Press.

Aron, L., and Starr, K. (2014). *A Psychotherapy for the people: Toward a Progressive Psychoanalysis*. New York: Rutledge.

Balint, M. (1932). Character analysis and the new beginning. In: *Primary Love and Psycho-Analytic Technique*, enl. ed. (pp. 151–164). London: Tavistock.

———. (1934). The final goal of psycho-analytic treatment. In: *Primary Love and Psycho-Analytic Technique*. enl. ed. (pp. 178–188). London: Tavistock.

Bayles, M. (2012). Is physical proximity essential to the psychoanalytic process? An exploration through the lens of Skype? *Psychoanalytic Dialogues*, 22, 569–585.

Bearison, D. J. and Zimiles, H. (1986). Developmental perspectives of thought and emotion: An introduction. In D. J. Bearison and H. Zimiles (Eds.). *Thought and Emotions: Developmental Perspectives* (pp1–10). Hillsdale, NJ: Erlbaum.

Beck, A. T. (1996). Beyond belief: A theory of modes, personality and psychopathology. In P. M. Salkovskis (Ed.), *Frontiers of Cognitive Therapy*. (pp. 1–25). New York, NY: Guilford Press.

Beebe, B. and Lachman, M. (2014). *The Origins of Attachment. Infant Research and Adult Treatment*. New York: Rutledge.

Benveniste, D. (1998). Play and the metaphor of the body. *The Psychoanalytic Study of the Child*, 53, pp.65–83. New Haven, CT: Yale University Press.

Blake, R. R. and Ramsey, G. V., (eds.) (1951). *Perception: An Approach to Personality.* New York: Ronald Press.
Blum, M. C. (2015). Embodied mirroring: A relational, body-to- body technique promoting movement in therapy. *Journal of Psychotherapy Integration*, 25, 115–127.
Bonaiuto, M. and Bonnes, M. (2000). Social-psychological approaches to environment-behavior studies: Identity theories and the discursive approach. In S. Wapner, J. Demick, T. Yamamoto, and H. Minami (Eds.). *Theoretical Perspectives in Environment-Behavior Research: Underlying Assumptions, Research Problems and Methodologies* (pp. 76–78). New York: Kluwer Academic/ Plenum Press.
Bornstein, R. F. (2001). The Impending Death of Psychoanalysis. *Psychoanalytic Psychology*, 18, 3–20.
Bronfenbrenner, U. and Morris, P. A. (2008). The bioecological model of human development. In W. Damon and R. M. Lerner (Eds.). *Handbook of Child Psychology: Vol 1. Theoretical Models of Human Development.* (pp. 793–828). Hoboken, NJ: Wiley Interscience.
Brown, F. (1958). The psychodiagnostic test battery. In D. Brown and L. E. Aby (Eds.), *Progress in Clinical Psychology* (pp. 60–71) New York: Grune & Stratton.
Bruner, J. S. (1951). Personality dynamics and the process of perceiving, In R. R. Blake and G. V. Ramsey (Eds.). *In Perception: An Approach to Personality.* (pp 121–147). New York: Ronald Press.
———. (1986). Thought and emotion: Can Humpty Dumpty be put back together again? In D. J. Bearison and H. Zimiles (Eds.). *Thought and Emotions: Developmental Perspectives.* (pp 11–20). Hillsdale, NJ: Erlbaum.
———. (1992). Another look at the New Look I. *American Psychologist*, 47, 780–785.
Bucci, W. (2000). The need for "Psychoanalytic Psychology" in the cognitive science field. *Psychoanalytic Psychology*, 17, 203–224.
Camic, P. M., Brooker, J. and Neal, A. (2011). Found objects in clinical practice: preliminary evidence. *The Arts in Psychotherapy*, 38, 151–159.
Campos, J. J., Frankl, C. B., and Camras, L. (2004). On the nature of emotion regulation. *Child Development*, 75, 377–394.
Cash, T. F. (2002). Beyond traits. Assessing body image states. In T. F. Cash and T. Pruzinsky (Eds.). *Body Image. A Handbook of Theory, Research and Clinical Practice* (pp 163–170). New York: Guildford Press.
Cash, T. F. and Pruzinsky (Eds.). (2002). *Body Image: A Handbook of Theory, Research and Clinical Practice.* New York: Guildford Press.
Cattell, R. B. (1957). *Personality and Motivation Structure and Measurement.* New York: World Book.
Colosimo, K. A. and Pos, A. E. (2015). A relational model of expressed therapeutic presence. *Journal of Psychotherapy Integration*, 25, 100–114.
Coppolillo, H. P. (1987). *Psychodynamic Psychotherapy of Children: An Introduction to the Art and Techniques.* Madison, CT: International Universities Press.
Costa, P. T. and Widger, T. A. (Eds.) (2004) *Personality Disorders and the Five Factor Model of Personality.* (2nd ed.). Washington, DC: American Psychological Association
Crandall, V. J. (1963). Achievement. In H. W. Stevenson (Ed.). *Child Psychology: The Sixty-Second Yearbook of the National Society of the Study of Education* (pp. 416–459). Chicago: University of Chicago Press.
Decarie, T. G. (1978). Affect development and cognition in a Piagetian context. In M. Lewis and L. A. Rosenblum (Eds.). *The Development of Affect.* (pp. 183–230). New York: Plenum Press.
Diamond, M. J. and Christian, C. (Eds.) (2011). *The Second Century of Psychoanalysis: Evolving Perspectives on Therapeutic Action.* London: Karnac Books.
Dodds, J. and Santostefano, S. (1964). A comparison of the cognitive functioning of glue-sniffers and non-glue sniffers. *Journal of Pediatrics*, 64, 565 570.
Dosamantes-Alperson, E. and Merrill, N. (1980). Growth effects of experiential movement psychotherapy. *Psychotherapy: Theory, Research and Practice*, 17, 63–68.

Eke, L. and Gent, A. M. (2010). Working with withdrawn adolescents as a moving experience: A community resourced project exploring the usefulness of group dance movement psychotherapy within a school setting. *Body Movement and Dance in Psychotherapy*, 5, 45–57.

Ellman, S. J. and Moskowitz, M. eds. (1998). *Enactment: Toward A New Approach to the Therapeutic Relationship*. Northvale, NJ: Aronson.

Erickson, E. H. (1950). *Childhood and Society*, 2nd ed. New York: W. W. Norton.

Fairbairn, W. R. D. (1958). On the nature and aims of psycho-analytic treatment. *International Journal of Psychoanalysis*, 39, 147–167.

Ferenczi, S. (1920). The further development of an active technique in psycho-analysis. *In Further Contributions to the Theory and Technique of Psycho-Analysis*. London: Hogarth Press, 1969, pp. 198–217.

———. (1931). Child analysis in the analysis of adults. *International Journal of Psychoanalysis*, 12, 468–471.

Ferenczi, S. and Rank, O. (1924). *The Development of Psychoanalysis*. Madison, CT: International Universities Press, 1980.

Flavell, J. H. (1963). *The Developmental Psychology of Jean Piaget*. New York: Van Nostrand.

Frank, K. A. (1999). *Psychoanalytic Participation: Action, Interaction and Integration*. Hillsdale, NJ: The Analytic Press.

———. (2002). The "ins and outs" of enactment: A relational bridge for psychotherapy integration. *Journal of Psychotherapy Integration*, 12, 267–286.

Freedman, N. (1977). Hands, words and mind: On the structuralization of body movements during discourse and the capacity for verbal representation. *In Communicative Structures and Psychic Structures*, N. Freedman and S. Grand (eds.). pp 109–132. New York: Plenum.

Freud, S. (1912). Recommendations to Physicians Practicing Psychoanalysis. *Standard Edition*, 12, 109–120. London: Hogarth Press, 1958.

———. (1914). Remembering, repeating and working-through (further recommendations on the technique of psychoanalysis: I). *Standard Edition* 12, 145–156.

Gabbard, G. O. and Weston, D. (2003). Rethinking Therapeutic Action. *International Journal of Psychoanalysis*, 84, 823–841.

Galton, F. (1884). Measurement of character. *The Forthnightly Review*, 36, 179–185.

Gardner, H. (1985). *The Mind's New Science: A History of the Cognitive Revolution*. New York: Basic Books.

Gill, W. (2010). Report of the 11th congress of the European Association for Body Psychotherapy. *Body Movement and Dance in Psychotherapy*, 5, 89–93.

Good, J. M. (2000). The affordances for social psychology of the ecological approach to social knowing. *Theory and Psychology*, 17, 265–295.

Greenberg, J. (1996). Psychoanalytic words and psychoanalytic acts: A brief history. *Contemporary Psychoanalysis*, 32, 195–213.

Greenson, R. R. (1965). The working alliance and the transference neurosis. *Psychoanalytic Quarterly*, 34, 155–181.

Grossmark, R. (2012). The flow of enactive engagement. *Contemporary Psychoanalysis*, 48, 287–300.

Gruber, H. E., Hammond, K. R. and Jesser, R. (Eds.) (1957). *Contemporary Approaches to Cognition*. Cambridge, MA: Harvard University Press.

Hanan, M. E. (2013). Embodied therapy for clients expressing gender variation: Using creative movement to explore and express body concerns. In L. Sana (ed.) *Expressive Therapies for Sexual Issues: A Social Work Perspective*, (pp. 1–38). New York, NY: Springer Science and Business Media.

Hart, R. and Rollins, J. (2011). *Therapeutic Activities for Children and Teens Coping with Health Issues*. Hoboken, NJ: John Wiley & Sons.

Harter, S. (1999). *The Construction of the Self: A Developmental Perspective*. New York: Guilford Press.

Hartman, H. (1939, published in German). *Ego Psychology and the Problem of Adaptation* (1st English ed.). New York: International Universities Press, 1958 (published in English).
Hersen, M. (Ed) (2003). *Comprehensive Handbook of Psychological Assessment*. Hoboken, NJ: John Wiley & Sons.
Hollin, C. R. (1990). *Cognitive-Behavioral Interventions with Young Offenders*. New York: Pergamon Press.
Holt, R. R. (1964). The emergence of cognitive psychology. *Journal of the American Psychoanalytic Association*, 12, 650–665.
Jacobs, T. J. (1991). *The Use of the Self*. Madison, CT: International Universities Press.
James, W. (1890). *Principles of Psychology*. Chicago: Encyclopedia Britannica.
Johansen, S. G., Wang, C. E. A., Binder, P. and Malt, U. F. (2014). Equine-facilitated body and emotion-oriented psychotherapy designed for adolescents and adults not responding to mainstream treatment: A structured program. *Journal of Psychotherapy Integration*, 24, 323–335.
Johnson, M. (2008). The meaning of the body. In W. F. Overton, U. Muller and J. L. Newman (Eds.). *Developmental Perspectives on Embodiment and Consciousness* (pp. 19–44). New York: Erlbaum.
Jones, E. E. (2000). *Therapeutic Action: A Guide to Psychoanalytic Therapy*. Northvale, NJ: Jason Aronson.
Jung, C. G. (1952). *Symbols of Transformation*. New York: Bollingen Foundation
Kagan, J. (2005). Temperament and personality. In M. Rosenbluth, S. H. Kennedy and M. F. Bagby (Eds,) *Depression and Personality: Conceptual and Clinical Challenges*. (pp. 3–18). Washington, DC: American Psychiatric Press.
Kramer, S. and Akhtar, S. (Eds.) (1992) *When the Body Speaks: Psychological Meanings in Kinetic Clues*. Northvale, NJ: Jason Aronson.
Knoblauch, S. H. (1997). Beyond the word in psychoanalysis: The unspoken dialogue. *Psychoanalytic Dialogues*, 7, 491–516.
Krantz, A. M. (2012). Let the body speak: Commentary on paper by Jon Sletvold. *Psychoanalytic Dialogues*, 22, 437–438.
Kring, A. M. and Sloan, D. M. (2007). The facial coding system (FACES): Development, validation, and utility. *Psychological Assessment*, 19, 210–224.
Lars-Gunnar, L. (2014). The search for common factors in psychotherapy: Two theoretical models with different empirical implications. *Psychology and Behavioral Sciences*, 3 (5), 131–150.
Lindzey, G. and Tejessy, C. (1956). TAT: Indices of aggression in relation to measures of overt and covert behaviors. *American Journal of Orthopsychiatry*, 26, 567–576.
Loewald, H. W. (1960). On the therapeutic action of psychoanalysis. In *Papers on Psychoanalysis*. New Haven, CT. Yale University Press, 1980, pp. 221–256.
London, P. (1964). *The Modes and Morals of Psychotherapy*. New York: Holt, Rinehart & Winston.
Mahl, G. F. (1987). *Explorations in Nonverbal and Vocal Behaviors*. Hillsdale, NJ: Erlbaum.
McLaughlin, J. T. (1991). Clinical and theoretical aspects of enactment. *Journal of the American Psychoanalytic Association*, 39, 595–614.
Meehums, B., Varemiece, L., Majore-Dusele, I, and Rasnacs, O. (2012). Dance movement therapy for obese women with emotional eating: A controlled pilot study. *The Arts in Psychotherapy*, 39, 126–133.
Megargee, E. D. (1965). Relations between barrier scores and aggressive behavior. *Journal of Abnormal Psychology*, 70, 307–311.
Messer, S. B. and Winokur, M. (1984). Ways of knowing and visions of reality in psychoanalytic therapy and behavior therapy. In H. Arkowitz and S. B. Messer (Eds). *In Psychoanalytic Therapy and Behavioral Therapy: Is Integration Possible?* (pp, 63–100): New York: Plenum.
Messer, S. B. and Woltsky, D. L. (2010). A psychodynamic perspective on the therapeutic alliance: Theory research and practice. In J. C. Muran and J. P., Barber (Eds.)

The Therapeutic Alliance: An Evidence-Based Guide to Practice. (97–122). New York: Guildford Press.

Miller, M. L. (2004). Dynamic systems and the therapeutic action of the analyst: II Clinical application and illustrations. *Psychoanalytic Psychology*, 21, 54–68.

Milner, M. (1981, October 26). Transcript of a tape-recorded interview conducted by James W. Anderson, copy in possession of James W. Anderson, Chicago.

Mitchell, S. A. (1994). Recent developments in psychoanalytic theorizing. *Journal of Psychotherapy Integration*, 4, 93–103.

Moscovitz, S. (2014). Hans Loewald's "On the therapeutic action of psychoanalysis": Initial reception and later influence. *Psychoanalytic Psychology*, 31, 575–587.

Munari, B. (2005). *Speak Italian. The Fine Art of Gesture. A Supplement to the Italian Dictionary*. San Francisco, CA. Cronicle Books

Newnham, E. A. and Page, A. C. (2010). Bridging the gap between best evidence and best practice in mental health. *Clinical Psychology Review*, 30, 127–142.

Overton, W. F. (1994). The arrow of time and the cycle of time: Concepts of change, cognition and embodiment. *Psychological Inquiry*, 5, 215–237.

———. (1998). Relational-developmental theory: A psychological perspective. In D. Gorlitz, H. J. Harloff, J. Valsiner, and G. Mey (Eds.) *Children, Cities and Psychological Theories: Developing Relationships.* (pp 73–102). New York: de Gruyer/Mouton.

———. (2004). Embodied development: Ending the nativism-empiricism debate. In C. Garcia Coll, E. Beaver and R. Lerner (Eds.) *Nature and Nurture: The Complex Interplay of Genetic and Environmental Influences on Human Behavior and Development.* (pp. 201–223) Mahwah, NJ: Lawrence Erlbaum Associates.

———. (2006). Developmental psychology: philosophy, concepts, methodology. In R. M. Lerner (Ed.), *Handbook of Child Psychology: Vol. I Theoretical Models of Human Development.* (6th ed.) (pp. 18–88). Hoboken, NJ: John Wiley & Sons.

Overton, W. F., Muller, V. and Newman, J. (Eds.) (2008). *Developmental Perspectives on Embodiment and Consciousness.* New York: Earlbaum.

Payne, H. (2009). Pilot study to evaluate dance movement psychotherapy (the body mind approach) in patients with medically unexplained symptoms: Participant and facilitator perceptions and a summary discussion. *Body Movement and Dance in Psychotherapy*, 4, 77–94.

Pearson, M. and Wilson, H. (2009). *Using Expressive Arts to Work with Mind, Body and Emotions: Theory and Practice.* London, UK: Jessica Kingsley Publishers.

Piaget, J. (1951). *Play, Dreams and Imitation in Childhood*. New York, Norton.

———. (1967). *Six Psychological Studies*. New York: Random House.

———. (1973). The Affective unconscious and the cognitive unconscious. *Journal of the American Psychoanalytic Association*, 21, 249–266.

———. (1975). Foreword. In E. J. Anthony (ed.) *Explorations in Child Psychiatry* (pp vii–ix). New York: Plenum

Pine, F. (1998) *Diversity and Direction in Psychoanalytic Technique*. New Haven, CT: Yale University Press.

Poulin, M., Haase, C. M. and Hechausen, J. (2005). Engagement and disengagement across the life span: an analysis of two-person models of developmental regulation. In W. Greve, K Rothermund, and O. Wentura (Eds.). *The Adaptive self: personal continuity and intentional self-development* (pp. 117–136). Ashland, OH: Hogrefe & Harber Publishers.

Pruzinsky, T. (1990). Somtopsychic approaches to psychotherapy and personal growth. In T. F. Cash and T. Pruzinsky (Eds.) *Body Images: Development, Deviance and Change* (pp. 296–315). New York: Guilford Press.

Pruzinsky, T. and Cash, T. F. (2002). Understanding body images: Historical and contemporary perspectives. In T. F. Cash and T. Pruzinsky (Eds.), *Body Image: A Handbook of Theory, Research and Clinical Practice.* (pp. 3–12). New York: Guildford Press.

Pylvanainen, P. (2008). A dance movement therapy group as a community outreach for intercultural women in Tokyo. *Body Movement and Dance in Psychotherapy*, 3, 31–44.

———. (2010). The dance movement therapy group in a psychiatric outpatient clinic: Explorations in body image and interaction. *Body Movement and Dance Psychrapyothe*, 5, 219–230.

Rabinor, J. R. and Bilich, M. (2011). Experiential approaches to body image change. In T. F. Cash and L. Smolak (Eds.) *Body Image: A Handbook of Science, Practice and Prevention* (2nd ed.) pp. 424–433. New York: Guilford Press.

Rader, G. E. (1957). The prediction of overt aggressive verbal behavior from the Rorshach content. *Journal of Professional Technology*, 21, 294–306.

Reinecke, M. A. and Freeman, A. (2007). Development and treatment of personality disorders: Summary. In A. Freeman and M. A. Reinecke (eds.) *Personality Disorders in Childhood and Adolescence.* (pp. 681–697), Hoboken, NJ: John Wiley & Sons.

Renick, O. (1998). The role of countertransference: Enactment in a successful clinical psychoanalysis. In S. J. Ellman and M. Moskowitz (Eds.) *Enactment: Toward a New Approach to the Therapeutic Relationship.* (pp. 98–125). Northvale, NJ: Aronson.

Ressler, A. (2009). Body mind treatment: Connecting to imprinted emotions and experiences. In M, Maine, W. N. Davis, and J. Shure (Eds.) *Effective Clinical Practice in the Treatment of Eating Disorders: The Heart of the Matter.* (pp. 145–159) New York: Rutledge/Taylor & Francis Group.

Rodman, F. R. (Ed.) (1987). *The Spontaneous: Selected Letters of D. W. Winnicott.* Cambridge, MA: Harvard University Press.

Rogers, R. F., Sales P. and Chabrol, H. (2010). Psychological functioning, media pressure and body dissatisfaction among college women. *European Review of Applied Psychology*, 60, 89–95.

Rohricht, F., Papadopoulos, N., Suzuki, I., and Phriebe, S. (2009). Ego pathology, body experience, and body psychotherapy in chronic schizophrenia. *Psychology and Psychotherapy: Theory, Research and Practice*, 82, 19–30.

Rottenberg, J. and Gross, J. J. (2007). Emotion and emotion regulation: a map for psychotherapy researchers. *Clinical Psychology: Science and Practice*, 4, 323–328.

Sako, T. (1997). Big school, small school revisited: A case study of a large-scale comprehensive high school based on the campus plan. In S. Wapner, J. Demick, Y. Takiji, and T. Takahashi (Eds.) *Handbook of Japan-United States Environment-Behavior Research: Toward A Transactional Approach* (pp. 273–282). New York: Plenum Press.

Sander, L. W. (1962) Issues in early mother-child interaction. *Journal of the American Academy of Child Psychology*, 3, 141–166.

———. (1964). Adaptive relationships in early mother-child interaction. *Journal of the American Academy of Child Psychiatry*, 3, 231–264.

———. (1987). A 25 year follow up: some reflections on personality development over the long term. *Infant Mental Health Journal*, 8, 210–2020.

———. (1989). Investigations of the infant and its caregiving environments as a biological system. In S. J. Greenspan and G. H. Pollack (Eds.), *The Course of Life* (2nd ed., pp 359–391). Madison, WI: International Universities Press.

Santostefano, S. (1960). An Exploration of Performance Measures of Personality. *Journal of Clinical Psychology*, 16, 373–377.

———. (1962). Miniature Situation Test as a Way of Interviewing Children. *Merrill Palmer Quarterly of Behavior and Development*, 8, 261–269.

———. (1964a) A developmental study of the cognitive control leveling-sharpening. *Merrill-Palmer Quarterly of Behavior and Development.* 10, 343–360.

———. (1964 b). Cognitive Controls and Exceptional States in Children. *Journal of Clinical Psychology*, 20, 213–218.

———. (1965a). Construct validity of the Miniature Situations Test I: The performance of public school children, orphaned and brain damaged children. *Journal of Clinical Psychology*, 21, 418–421.

———. (1965b). Relating self-report and overt behavior: the concept of levels of modes for expressing motives. *Perceptual Motor Skills*, 21, 940.

———. (1968a). Miniature situations and methodological problems in parent-child interaction research. *Merrill-Palmer Quarterly of Behavior and Development*, 14, 285–312.

———. (1968b). Situational testing in personality assessment. In D. L. Sills (Ed.) *International Encyclopedia of the Social Sciences.* (pp. 48–55) New York. MacMillan Co. and The Free Press.

———. (1970). Assessment of motives in children. *Psychological Reports*, 26, 639–649.

———. (1971). Beyond nosology: Diagnosis from the viewpoint of development. In H. E. Rie (Ed.) *Perspectives in Child Psychopathology* (pp. 130–177). New York: Aldine-Atherton Co.

———. (1977). Action, fantasy and language: developmental levels of ego organization in communicating drives and affects. In N. Freedman and S. Grand (eds.). *Communicative Structures and Psychic Structures.* (pp. 331–356) New York: Plenum.

———. (1978). *A Biodevelopmental Approach to Clinical Child Psychology: Cognitive Controls and Cognitive Control Therapy*. New York: Wiley.

———. (1980). Cognition in personality and the treatment process: a psychoanalytic view. *Psychoanalytic Study of the Child*, 35, 41–46.

———. (1985). Metaphor: an integration of action, fantasy and language in development. *Imagination, Cognition and Personality*, 4, 127–146.

———. (1986). Cognitive controls, metaphors and contexts: an approach to cognition and emotion. In D. Bearison and H. Zimiles (Eds), *Thought and Emotion* (pp. 175–210) Hills dale, NJ: Erlbaum.

———. (1988). *The Cognitive Control Battery*. Los Angeles: Western Psychological Services.

———. (1992). *The Action Test of Body Image: Manual of Instructions and Scoring*. (Unpublished manuscript).

———. (1994). The arrow of time and developmental psychopathology. *Psychological Inquiry*, 5, 248–253.

———. (1995). Embodied meanings, cognition and emotion: probing how three are one. In D. Cicchetti and S. L. Toth (Eds.) *Rochester Symposium on Developmental Psychopathology. Vol. 6. Emotion, Cognition and Representation.* (pp. 59–132) Rochester, NY: University of Rochester Press.

———. (1998a). Cycles in the life of one psychotherapist. In J. Reppen (Ed.) *Why I Became a Psychotherapist.* (pp 237–248). Northvale, NJ: Jason Aronson.

———. (1998b) *A Handbook of Interactive Psychotherapies for Children and Adolescents.* Northvale, NJ: Jason Aronson.

———. (2004). *Child Therapy in the Great Outdoors: A Relational View*. Hillsdale, NJ: TheAnalytic Press.

———. (2010). Developmental psychopathology. Self, embodiment, meaning: A holistic-systems perspective. In W. F.Overton (Ed.) *The Handbook of Life-Span Development. Volume I: Cognition, Biology and Methods.* (pp. 792–836) Hoboken, NJ: Wiley.

———. (2012). *First to Last Picking. Sicilians in America, Yesterday, Today and Tomorrow.* Mineola, NY: Legas Press.

———. (2015). A psychodynamic, action-oriented method to assess the contributions of a person's body image to personality functioning. *Psychoanalytic Psychology*, 32, 255–274.

Santostefano, S. and Berkowitz, S. (1976). Principles of infant development as a guide in the psychotherapeutic treatment of borderline and psychotic children, *McLean Hospital Journal*, 1, 236–261.

Santostefano, S. and Calicchia, J. (1992). Body image, relational psychoanalysis and the construction of meaning: implications for treating aggressive children. *Development and Psychopathology*, 4, 655–678.

Santostefano, S. and Moncata, S. (1989). A psychoanalytic view of cognition within personality: cognitive dysfunction and educating troubled youth. *Residential Treatment for Children and Youth*, 6, 41–62.

Santostefano, S., MacAuley, L., O'Connell, B., Quiroga-Estevez, M., Santostefano, S. R., and Burke, P. (2006). What abandoned children construe as stressful experiences: implications for psychoanalytic relational theory and child psychotherapy. *Journal of Infant, Child and Adolescent Psychotherapy*, 5, 1–23.

Santostefano, S. and Reider, C. (1984). Cognitive controls and aggression in children: the concept of cognitive-affective balance. *Journal of Consulting and Clinical Psychology*, 52, 46–56.

Santostefano, S. and Wilson, S. (1968). Construct Validity of the Miniature Situations Test: II The Performance of Institutionalized Delinquents and Public School Adolescents. *Journal of Clinical Psychology*, 24, 355–358.

Sarason, I. G. and Sarason, B. R. (1981). The importance of cognition and moderator variables. In D. Magonusson (Ed.). *Toward a Psychology of Situations: An Interpersonal Perspective*. (pp.195–210). Hillsdale, NJ: Erlbaum.

Shilder, P. (1935). *The Image and Appearance of the Human Body*. New York: International Universities Press.

Skinner, B. F. (1974). *About Behaviorism*. New York: Knopf.

Sletvold, J. (2012). Training analysts to work with unconscious embodied expressions: Theoretical underpinnings and practical guidelines. *Psychoanalytic Dialogues*, 22, 410–429.

———. (2014) *The Embodied Analyst. From Freud and Reich to Relationality*. London and New York: Rutledge.

Sokol, B. W. and Muller, U. (2007). The development of self-regulation: Toward the integration of cognition and emotion. *Cognitive Development*, 22, 401–405.

Stern, D. N. (1985) *The Interpersonal World of the Infant: A View from Psychoanalysis and Developmental Psychology*. New York: Basic Books.

Stern, D. N., Sander, L. W., Nahum, J. P., Harrison, A. M., Lyons-Ruth, K., Morgan, A. C., Brunschweilerston, N. and Tronick, E. Z. (1998) Non-interpretative mechanisms in psychoanalytic therapy: The something more than interpretation. *International Journal of Psychoanalysis*, 79, 903–921.

Stern, S. (2002). Identification, repetition and psychological growth. *Psychoanalytic Psychology*, 19, 722–738.

Stoops, J. W. (1974). The assessment of aggression in children: arguments for a multimodal approach. Unpublished doctoral dissertation, Kent State University, Kent, OH.

Sullivan, H. S. (1953). *The Interpersonal Theory of Psychiatry*. New York: W. W. Norton & Co.

Summers, F. (2001). What I do with what you give me: Therapeutic action is the creation of meaning. *Psychoanalytic Psychology*, 18, 635–655.

Swift, J. K. and Greenberg, R. P. (2012). Premature discontinuation in adult psychotherapy: A meta-analysis. *Journal of Consulting and Clinical Psychology*, 80, 547–559.

Symonds, P. M. (1931). *Diagnosing Personality and Conduct*. New York: Appleton-Century-Crofts.

Teachman, B. A., Stefanucci, J. K., Clerkin, E. M., Cody, M. W. and Proffitt, D. R. (2008). A new mode of fear expression: Perceptual bias in height fear. *Emotion*, 8, 296–301.

Thompson, J. K. and van der Berg, P. (2002). Measuring body image attitudes among adolescents and adults. In T. F. Cash and T. Pruzinsky (Eds.). *Body Image: A Handbook of Theory, Research and Clinical Practice* (pp. 142–154). New York: Guilford Press.

Toronto, E. L. K. (2001). The human touch: An exploration of the role and meaning of physical touch in psychoanalysis: Initial reception and later influence. *Psychoanalytic Psychology*, 31, 575–587.

Tracy, J. L. and Robins, R. W. (2007). The prototypical pride expression: Development of a nonverbal coding system. *Emotion*, 7, 789–801.

Wachtel, P. L. (1987). *Action and Insight*. New York: Guilford Press.

Waldholz, M. (2003, August 26). Flower power: How gardens improve your mental health. *The Wall Street Journal*.

Wapner, S. and Demick, J. (2000). Assumptions, methods and research problems of the holistic, developmental, systems-oriented perspective. In S. Wapner, J. Demick, T. Yamomoto, and H. Minami (Eds.). *Theoretical Perspectives in Environment-Behavior Research: Underlying Assumptions, Research Problems and Methodologies* (pp. 7–19). New York: Klumer Academic/Plenum Press.

Weinberg, H. (2010). Using art therapy technique in a psychodynamic-oriented group. In S. S. Fehr (Ed.) *101 Interventions in Group Therapy* (rev. ed.) (pp. 145–149) New York: Routledge/Taylor & Francis Group.

Werner, H. (1957). The concept of development from a comparative and organismic point of view. In D. B. Harris (ed.) *The Concept of Development: An Issue in the Study of Human Behavior*. (pp. 125–148). Minneapolis: University of Minnesota Press.

———. (1964). *Comparative Psychology of Mental Development*, rev. ed. New York: International Universities Press.

Wiener, D. J. (Ed). (1999). *Beyond Talk Therapy: Using Movement and Expressive Techniques in Clinical Practice.* Washington, DC: American Psychological Association.

Wolfe, B. E. (2003). Knowing the self: Building a bridge from basic research to clinical practice. *Journal of Psychotherapy Integration*, 13, 83–95.

Wolff, W. (1943). *The Expression of Personality Experimental Depth Psychology*. New York: Harper and Brothers.

Yanover, T. and Thompson, J. K. (2009) Assessment of body image in children and adolescents. In L. Smolak and J. K. Thompson (Eds.) *Body Image, Eating Disorders, Obesity in Youth: Assessment, Prevention and Treatment* (2nd ed., pp177–192). Washington, DC: American Psychological Association.

Young, C. (2010). The history and development of body-psychotherapy: European diversity. *Body Movement and Dance in Psychotherapy*, 5, 5–19.

Index

About the Author

For many years Sebastiano Santostefano, PhD, ABPP, has made contributions teaching and training predoctoral and postdoctoral clinical psychology students and psychiatric residents, and designing diagnostic tests, developing treatment programs, and conducting and publishing research. Initially he held a faculty position at the University of Colorado School of Medicine and then at Clark University. Then while serving on the faculty of Boston University School of Medicine, he completed training in child and adult psychoanalysis at the Boston Psychoanalytic Institute. In 1972 he was asked to organize an outpatient and inpatient clinical program at McLean Hospital, served as director of the department and also as Associate Professor of Psychology, Department of Psychiatry, Harvard University Medical School. While in this position he also organized predoctoral and postdoctoral clinical psychology programs, provided courses to psychiatric residents, and conducted research. He resigned from this position in 1992 to organize and direct a nonprofit program that provided free services in community schools to children and adolescents who had witnessed or endured trauma and provided training to predoctoral and postdoctoral students. He continued conducting research and also assisted in designing a therapeutic garden described in a *New York Times* article in 2005. Currently he is semiretired, in part-time private practice and continues to publish articles.

www.ingramcontent.com/pod-product-compliance
Ingram Content Group UK Ltd.
Pitfield, Milton Keynes, MK11 3LW, UK
UKHW041626031026
15587UKWH00001B/100

9 781498 561006